WAMPANOAG MORNING

Stories from the Land of the People of the First Light Before the English Invasion

MANITONQUAT (MEDICINE STORY)

authorHOUSE®

AuthorHouse™
1663 Liberty Drive, Suite 200
Bloomington, IN 47403
www.authorhouse.com
Phone: 1-800-839-8640

First published by AuthorHouse 11/3/2008

ISBN: 978-1-4389-0010-0 (sc)

Printed in the United States of America
Bloomington, Indiana

This book is printed on acid-free paper.

DEDICATION

*To our young people of the Wampanoag and Wabanaki
and to all our young people, and to the unborn generations to come, Native and non-
Native, who will struggle to deal with the world and the cultures we have left them,
that they may learn and remember the wisdom of earlier times, times when life was
grounded in the earth and the natural world and the turning of the seasons, when
the people lived in circles of relationship and cooperation, and the Spirit of Creation
was not distant and obscure but practical and real and present in every moment.*

The story Apponaug was written for the daughters of my friend Slow Turtle and Burne Stanley Peters. The Story of Epanow was dedicated to Chief Windsong Alden Blake of the Assonet Wampanoag on the occasion of the opening of our community house on the Watuppa Wampanoag Reservation. I would like to dedicate the Legend of Weetucks to our young elder gkisedtanamoogk and to the memory of our dedicated sub-chief Nanepashemet.

INTRODUCTION

This is a group of stories taking place in the country of my people, the Wampanoag, in the times before the invasion of the Pilgrims and the Puritans. Wampanoag country is and was bounded on the north by the Massachuset, on the west by the Nipmuc, on the south by the Narragansett, and on the east by the ocean. That land, extending from Bristol, Rhode Island to just below the Blue Hills of Boston, Massachusetts, was sometimes referred to as Pokonoket, land of Salt Water Bays, and includes Cape Cod and the Islands. Young people, elders and teachers may recognize that the central characters are young people who are at the time of coming into adulthood, a time for which our people would traditionally be given a welcoming ceremony by the elders.

I have already told many legends of our people in a book called <u>Children of the Morning Light,</u> I wrote them in the way that I tell them so they may be understood by young and old. The stories in this book are written more for adults and more advanced young people. I have told them in this way to give a picture of how life was before the invasion of the Europeans, and also to consider the culture and its wisdom of those times as we regard the cultures of today.

The first two stories are based on legends. Perhaps I should distinguish here among the words legend, myth, tale, and story. A story, states Webster's Unabridged, is a "connected narration of that which has occurred, a description of past events...In Literature, a narrative in either prose or verse...especially a fictitious narrative." A story may be true or fictitious, a tale is usually considered to be fiction, "story" being the more general word and "tale" being often elevated or poetical. Myths and legends are tales from the past, the origin of which is forgotten often explaining some belief or practice or phenomenon, and are transmitted through a whole culture. In common usage, myths are more likely to involve gods and magic and fabulous creatures, while legends are more likely to relate the actions of human beings, heroic perhaps, but mostly conforming to the laws of nature we currently accept.

"The Legend of Weetucks" is a retelling of that legend of my people, which touches myth at the end upon Weetucks' departure, in a storyteller's mode of re-imagining the events and elaborating upon them, and using that story to comment upon the situation facing young Native people of today.

"Wolf Dreamer" is also a legend which has a slight coloration of magic, but a magic that can be interpreted as you please, which I have retold as a story to breathe a bit more life into it and comment on the truth to be found in tales.

"Wequash's World" re-imagines the account in the Vinland Sagas of Iceland of the encounters between Vikings and Native people in North America in the eleventh century as they might have been seen and told by the natives in that time.

"Apponaug" is an idyllic imagining of life among the Nausets on the outer arm of Cape Cod in the early sixteenth century, based upon the stories and practices which have been handed down through oral traditions. It concludes with musings by the young people over the story of pale hairy beings from some other world that appeared to their neighbors to the south and a strange foreboding of the future.

"The Day the Magic Disappeared" is again a retelling from a Native perspective of an historical event known to us only through the reports of the invading French explorers.

Finally, "The Story of Epanow" – the only story in which the central character has already attained adulthood - is a narration of an actual historical event, which through the retelling during more than three hundred and seventy years has taken on mythical and magical trappings. I have cast the story in a way that might also be acceptable to those young people of today who may have a skeptical attitude about mythology.

Three of these stories are told in the voice of contemporary storytellers, as I might myself tell them (and often do). That's an old-fashioned form, but I hope you don't have a problem with it, because it's the form I choose to reflect upon their relevance to our contemporary world and the problems we Native people have in dealing with it.

Contents

THE LEGEND OF WEETUCKS

1. Prologue

The old storyteller was on his way through the woods to the sacred circle when he saw a group of young people sitting by themselves off to one side of the path.

"You coming to the ceremonies?" he asked them.

Two of the younger boys got up to follow him, but stopped when they saw the others did not rise to the invitation. The old storyteller regarded them all.

"It seems," he said, "the ceremonies don't interest you so much."

"They're boring," one of the more outspoken girls offered. The other girls giggled, but the oldest boy shook his head, as if to disown such disrespect.

"Well, they are," she went on. "We are supposed to tell the truth, aren't we?"

"You are right to speak out. Why are they boring, do you think?"

"There's nothing for kids to do," one of the smaller boys said.

"They just sit in a circle and talk all the time," another girl said.

"And what do you do together here?" the storyteller asked.

"Talk!" The oldest boy spoke up, and they all laughed.

"Nothing."

"Tell jokes."

"There's nothing to do here."

"What would you do at home?" The storyteller persisted.

"Watch TV."

"Play video games."

"Go to the mall."

"Want to come with me?" the storyteller looked around at young faces growing interested and curious. "I want to show you something."

"What is it?"

"A rock."

"Profile Rock?" "Council Rock?" "Anawon's Rock?"

"I call it Weetuck's Rock, but today it's known as Dighton Rock. Have any of you seen it?" They shook their heads. "Come on then. It's something to do. And there's a story."

"Let's go!"

They all piled into the storyteller's old van, and off they went down the back roads of southeastern Massachusetts to Dighton Rock State Park. There, by the river, was a small stone house which sheltered the rock. But before they went in to see it, the old storyteller made a circle with them by the river.

"We will have our own ceremonies here," he said. The young people looked at each other.

"What do we do?"

"First we will burn some sweet grass." The old man took a braid of long grass and set one end on fire. When he blew out the flame the grass continued to smoke, and he brought it around for each one to smell, waving the smoke around them with an eagle feather.

"Does anyone know why we do this smudging?"

"To purify ourselves?"

"Hmm. So many people say. And what does that mean, do you think?"

The boy who had spoken shrugged.

"That's all right. It probably means different things to different people. What I think is that when we burn a special plant or herb, like sweet grass or cedar, the smell reminds us that this is a special time, a sacred time for thinking of sacred things. It reminds us to give our greetings and our thanksgivings to our Mother Earth, who provides all we need to live, to all of her children, the plant people, animal, fish, bird and insect people, who are our relatives, to all the distant unknown relatives through the great universe, and to the power that put all of that there, and gave us our lives, which let us be together at this time-the one our people call Kiehtan, the Creator. So be it our minds."

"Ho!" the young people said at once.

"What do we do now?" asked the girl who said ceremonies were boring.

"What do you want? This is your ceremony."

"The story!" They all cried.

For you know above almost all else, no matter what their age, all people love a good story. And so the storyteller began his tale.

2. The Woman of the Woods

Our people have always known how to live well and be happy. This they learned in the very morning of the world from first-teacher Maushop. He taught that all of Creation is one harmony, a circle. Therefore, he said, human beings must also live in harmony with themselves, with each other, with all other beings, and with Metta-n'okit, Our Mother the Earth. He taught that to maintain that harmony the center of the human circle must be respected. And he gave us ceremonies so that we could pass that knowledge to future generations.

After Maushop went beyond where the sun rises and left the world in our keeping, the people lived for a long time according to the ways that he had taught. Generation after generation came and went like the waves that follow each other to the shore. But it happened at last that although the Song of Creation was still sung, and the stories of Maushop were still told, people began to neglect the ceremonies.

At first they forgot to explain to the young people about the ceremonies and to bring them through rites of passage to manhood and womanhood. And so after a while these rituals became merely a duty, an empty practice without meaning. Of course, young people soon find boring the practices they do not understand which seem to them meaningless duties. As new generations came the ceremonies which had been neglected became forgotten.

Then the people did not come together so often, and when they did they did not consider the meaning of harmony and respect and the great wheels of the universe, of sun and moon and Mother Earth. They no longer held all things sacred and began to consider only themselves and their own desires more and more. Instead of love and sharing, the people sank into jealousy and greed. They no longer honored and cared for their elders and the little ones. When they did come together they only gossiped and gambled and told wicked stories about others behind their backs.

Now there was a young woman in one of our villages who felt in her heart that this was wrong. She had heard stories from her grandmother when she was little, about how life in the village used to be so happy and harmonious. But instead of caring and fun what she encountered growing up was scorn and mockery. It became harder and harder for her to live there. But rather than criticize, which would have been disrespectful, she decided only to leave the village and live in her own way by herself in the forest.

She knew how to cut and strip saplings and bury their ends in a circle in the earth, and to bend them over and bind them together in a dome, which she covered with bark. She made mats of reeds and grasses and wooden splints woven together and lined the inside of her house with these. She dug a tunnel to bring

3

air from outside under the ground to the fire pit in the center of her lodge to keep her fire brisk and bright and push the smoke upward to her smoke hole in the top.

She knew how to speak to fish in the streams. With a prayer she planted the three sisters, corn, beans, and squash. She knew how to gather wild foods, nuts and berries and roots and leaves that were good to eat. She knew how to make and set traps for small animals, and how to make her clothing and tools from skin, bone, and sinew. And so she lived simply in the peaceful cycles of the ancient forest and was content.

Naturally the other people of her village thought that she was strange, perhaps even crazy, for wanting to live alone and apart from all they knew. Being always absent she was the subject of much gossip and ridicule. Seeing her sometimes wandering about gathering herbs and singing the old songs, they suspected she might be practicing magic. They feared witchcraft, as it might be directed against themselves, and when someone got sick they wondered if she might be the cause, and there was argument about whether to go to her for a cure, or whether to kill or drive her away. In the end, out of fear of the unknown, they did neither. If anyone had managed to overcome this fear and go to her for a healing, no doubt she would have gladly treated him, for she was a kind hearted person, and she had learned much in ways and uses of herbs and roots. After one cure people might have trusted her, and she would have become known as a medicine woman.

But another thing happened to cause even more gossip and speculation about her. After some time it became very apparent that the woman was carrying a child. Of course the first question in everyone's mind was who the father might be. All men in the village were under suspicion. If one of the men had been absent he would have been whispered about. Wives watched their husbands carefully, and the young men watched each other. Some people suspected it must be a stranger, someone from another village, or even a traveler from a far land. Yet no man was ever seen in her company, no stranger ever noticed in the area.

Then the witch stories began to grow again. Perhaps the father was a sorcerer she had met in some magical journey on the dark winds. Or perhaps a demon she had conjured from the night. One person had seen a lone black wolf in the forest and heard its doleful baying, and suggested it could be a shape-shifter. All waited to see what kind of cub this sorcerer woman would bear.

3. The Wonderful Child

No one witnessed the birth of the child. The woman did not send for a relative or elder woman to help. Perhaps she had not enough time. In any case, it seemed she needed no help, and soon the villagers noticed that she carried a newborn on her back. When she walked she propped the baby up in the cradleboard, or hung it from a branch of a tree to sway gently in the breeze. The baby, like all our little ones, seemed very cozy and content, wrapped in the safe comfort of the cradleboard, which our people call "our grandmother."

It was a boy, this little child, and the woman named him Weetucks. He was, as we all were as newborns, a sweet and lovable baby, and very lively and curious, and his mother loved him greatly. She was very attentive to him, as though she knew already that he was a very special being that had been entrusted to her by Creation. She took him everywhere with her. When he lay in his cradleboard outside he would watch the birds and sing their songs back to them, and reach out to the little chipmunks and squirrels and rabbits that came to visit. When he began to crawl he would explore the world around him, touching smelling, listening, watching the butterflies, the ants, the ladybugs, the honeybees visiting the wild flowers. He seemed to know their languages, for soon he began to talk and to tell the stories they told him.

"Those termites are very upset now, Mama," he told her one day as they trooped past him on the ground. "After all their work to clear a place in that tree for their village, the woodpecker is digging it out for his own nest. Now they have decided to move to that rotten stump over there." His mother smiled, but saw in wonder the line of insects that crawled into the old stump.

Sometimes he would look up when the crows flew crying overhead and would call back to them in a voice like theirs, or he would squawk at the blue jays fussing about the bushes, and would report to his mother the news they brought.

Because his mother allowed him full freedom to explore his environment freely, it seemed his curiosity grew with each discovery. He crawled about and around the wetu that was their home, and to the edges of the meadow before it. Soon, earlier than most children his age, Weetucks was walking and climbing and digging and running. He began to range farther into the forest, visiting the homes of the woodchuck, the raccoon, the skunk, the badger, and the weasel. He brought home stories they told him of the ways of the woodlands. Muskrat taught him to swim, and he dove down with beaver to enter the underwater door to his house in the pond.

"Do you know what beaver does for fun?" Weetucks asked his mother, "He fells great trees. Just to watch them come crashing down. And to strengthen his jaw. Those trees are too big for him to use, but so much fun to bring down."

"And you know this because -?"

"He told me. And he showed me some medicine ways too. Beaver medicine is very strong. He got it from Maushop. People don't know once beaver was very big - like a monster - and Maushop had to make him small so he wouldn't smash everything. But he gave him powerful medicine in return. Human people do not come to learn from Beaver any more, but he says he will teach me."

Soon Weetucks began to bring plants home from his exploration of the meadows and forests. In his tiny fists he would be clutching flowers, herbs, roots, nuts, seeds, and bark, and he would spread them before his mother and tell her how and for what they could be used.

"This is for lungs," he might say, "Make it in a tea, and drink much of it for a cough. And this one – you can heat it in water then wrap it on an infection or a sore to pull out the poison. Now these flowers here may be eaten just as they are, and they are very healthy for the eyes. The seeds have special power because the whole plant is in them."

"How do you know all this?" she would ask.

"The plants themselves tell me." She asked how that happens.

"When I feel that a plant has a story to tell," he said, "I sit by it very quietly. If I am patient enough the plant will know it, and will speak to my mind and tell me of its powers."

He also told stories that the animals and birds had told him, about life in the forest, and the instructions which Creator had given their ancestors. So as he grew through his childhood he grew in knowledge and understanding, for he had many teachers.

His immense curiosity took him, when he could make his way by himself, into the village. His mother had told him that once she lived there but had left because she preferred the forest and the company of animal and bird friends to the company of men. She did not prevent his going to find her old home and form his own opinions of life there. Weetucks spent four days and three nights in the village, in order to discover the ways of village life and to speak to each person of every age, young and old. He played their gambling games with them and listened to their gossip. When he returned his mother asked about his journey, and he answered that he had learned nothing interesting there. That was at the end of his eighth summer.

When he was in his ninth summer he had an important dream in which a wolf came to him. He dreamed he was sitting on a high hill looking out over a forest and a lake and a river running through marshes to the sea. As he filled himself with the beauty of the scene he felt a warm presence beside him and turned to see a huge gray wolf looking at him with intense black eyes flecked with the blue of sky. In a voice that was not an animal sound but like the whisper of

6

wind in the trees and the swirling of water over stones the wolf told him that the forest would one day be in great danger, and not only this forest, but all the forests of the earth would be threatened with total destruction. When that happened many precious plants would disappear and all the animals and many human beings would have no place to go. In the dream was a vision of earth as lonely rock and sand and lifeless waters swept by empty winds.

The wolf told Weetucks that he had not many more seasons to learn as a child. Then he would become a man and teach the things that must be known to save their way of life. Weetucks' mother listened solemnly as he told his dream. She had always told him to pay attention and remember his dreams, for as you know, dreams are very important to our people. Sometimes dreams arise from problems we think about, or from feelings we have. Sometimes they refer to events of the past, and sometimes they show pictures of possible futures. Always they have something to teach us.

Weetucks wondered what this dream might mean, and his mother said she thought he was being told to prepare for something important he must do. He could not imagine what that might be, but she said he would know when the time came.

4. The Coming of Age

Seasons came and went, and Weetucks continued to listen to the voices of the forest world and to grow in stature and understanding. One day, early in his twelfth summer, Weetucks came to his mother and told her it was time for his initiation into manhood.

He went to a stand of willow and asked the willow chief for the gift of sixteen saplings. He left an offering of new tobacco leaves that he had grown for gifting and thanksgiving. He set the end of these saplings firmly into a circle in the ground. In the center he dug a little pit. Then he bent the saplings over and tied them in pairs across the circle until he had made a little dome. It was like the wetu where they lived, but much, much smaller, just big enough for a young boy ready to crawl out into manhood. He covered the little lodge with elk and moose robes and closed the door with a bearskin.

Then he built a fire and placed stones into the flames. When they were hot and glowing red he took forked sticks and carried the stones to the pit inside. Then he closed the bearskin door, and sat quietly in the dark. He thanked the glowing stones and the trees and the animals that made the little lodge. As he poured a little water on the stones they hissed and gave off much steam. Then he sang some special songs, which only he knew.

Weetucks sang to the fire outside, to the water and the winds. He sang to the earth on which he sat. He sang to Grandmother Moon, to Grandfather Sun, and to all the unknown star nations in the great universe beyond. The sweat poured out of his body, and there in the dark he felt as though he had left the world and gone where there was no time or space. He prayed towards the four directions to be cleansed in his body, in his thoughts, in his feelings, and in his soul. When he thought of the wolf's warning he wept and prayed for the protection of the great forest and all her children.

His mother had watched him build this lodge. She had gotten used to his coming home with knowledge that neither she nor any other human being had taught him. Even so, she was thrice astonished at this. She was surprised that he knew about a boy's initiation into manhood in the old ways, that he was to purify himself and then stay alone in the forest for a period of days, or even weeks. She was astonished that he knew how to build the purification lodge, or pesuponk, as the old ones had called it. And she was completely amazed to find he knew the ritual and the right songs to sing. She kept the fire for him while he made his purification and gave him parched corn and journey-cakes she had made for his quest into the forest. Then he was gone.

Well, I am sure she missed him right away. Before he was born she had lived alone in the great forest for many years, and she could manage well without him. But she had gotten used to his company. She wondered, as he grew, what surprise each new day would bring. What marvelous discovery he would relate to her when he came home every night. Now the nights went by all the same without any stories of a new adventure to make her laugh or shake her head in wonder.

It had been the dark of a new moon when he had purified himself in the pesuponk and disappeared northward, into the deep forest. Nanepaushet, Grandmother Moon, had grown and bathed the glade with her full glory, and then wrapped her dark shawl around her and hid her face once more. The woman had no concern that her son was alone for such a long time. She had heard stories from her mother's grandmother when she was very small, stories of boys of the older times, in the days of the elders, who stayed out for initiation as long as the time from new moon to new moon. And Weetucks knew the forest, was a creature of the forest himself. He had knowledge and he had power. He had strong dreams, and the spirits talked to him. And she knew in her heart that Creation had some important task for Weetucks and would protect him.

But when Nanepaushet began to grow and began to show her face again, the woman began to worry. This was too long a time for him to be on his quest. She waited one more night, and the next day she went to the village to seek help.

When they heard of Weetucks' decision to make his own initiation to manhood and to seek a vision in the forest, the older people were also astonished. They could recall stories, told them by their grandparents, of the long ago people doing what Weetucks was doing. No one now knew how to do that anymore, but here was this twelve-year-old boy doing this without being taught, and they marveled.

They all agreed, however, that he was gone too long. Something must have happened. Perhaps he had gotten lost and wandered off the edge of the world. Perhaps some monster or demon had devoured him.

"No," the boy's mother assured them, "Weetucks knows the forest and all the creatures in it. He would not get lost, and none would harm him."

"We must take a hunting team and try to track him," the village sachem said. Some of the young men looked uneasy. This was a witch-woman. Perhaps it was a trick to lure them to a trap. And the boy was probably a witch too. Certainly he had power, and those who have power are to be feared. The hunters all tried to look bold and unconcerned, but in their hearts they were afraid they might be eaten.

They took their dogs, and the dogs were excited but shared no signs of fear, so the men felt better. If Weetucks had become a serpent-person the dogs would whine and run away. But they found the boy's scent at the woman's house and scampered off on his trail. After a while the trail led into the river, and the dogs could not find it again. Then the men set loose their hunting falcons, and the birds soared up and down the stream and ranged in a wide circle over the trees, but at last returned without finding the trail of the boy.

"It is as we said," the hunters told the sachem, "Either the boy wandered too far and is in another land, or some animal has eaten him."

Or, thought some, he became a serpent-person and is living at the bottom of the river, ready to drag us down if we take our canoes there. Or, thought others, he is invisible and laughs at us even now, waiting until night to take us one by one down under the earth to be his winter food.

But in the morning they found him. Weetucks was lying on the path to the spring just outside of the village. He was unconscious, but alive, although he seemed very thin and all his body below his head was covered with dirt. When the sachem touched him, he woke right away, but was too weak to get up. So they carried him to the village and laid him in an empty wetu that no one used. The people were afraid to bring him into one of their own homes, afraid he might have a disease, or that some spirit was attacking him and might follow him into their lodges, or that he might be a witch-boy or sorcerer or even a half-demon trying to trick them.

"This boy is just starving," his mother said when she came. "Anyone can see that." So she moved into the wetu to nurse him back to his strength. After Weetucks had lain in the village for a night and nothing terrible had happened, curiosity overcame superstitious fears and, following the courageous example of their sachem, the village people began to come round with food, and soon the boy was strong enough to tell his story.

5. The Wisdom of Mettan'okit

When he left on his journey, Weetucks told them, he had determined not to hunt the creatures of the forest, only listen and observe and learn from them. After he had eaten his journey-cakes he looked for berries, but then he thought, "No, I will not take even the life of these. I will drink water from the springs and streams, but I will eat only sunshine and wind."

Soon he came to the salty stream our people called Titicut, where the dogs had lost his trail, he entered the water and lay floating on his back as the current carried him to the estuary and the ebbing tide left him on a muddy bank. There on the marshes he lay, in the waving eelgrass, by the salt pools, among the crab people. Rock crabs and blue crabs from the deep bay beyond came to lay eggs by the shore and to shed their old shells. Little pink crabs and some so tiny they seemed transparent, and shy hermit crabs outgrowing other people's borrowed shells, coming to find a larger one to inhabit. And whole tribes of busy fiddler crabs coming and going, always on the move. He listened to them all and began to learn the ways of the marsh, the delta, the bay and the sandy and rocky shores of the sound and the mysteries of the great sea beyond.

As he told his story, more and more people came to listen, for the people always love a good story. When the wetu became too full, Weetucks asked them to bring him outside where the whole village could hear. Then everyone came, and sat, and listened.

After staying a while with the marsh cabs, he had traveled to high ground to sit on the tallest hill he could find. There he could see the circle of the earth behind and of the sea before him. Now he began to meet bird people he had not known in the forest. He heard little terns darting from the beaches and back, and listened to their stories of the worlds they knew. He watched the passing of tribes of swans and geese and brants and ducks, and heard their tales of far-off lands. He talked with puffins and gannets and fish-hawks who spoke of distant rivers and islands, of ice floating in the sea, and the many tribes of great whales that roamed the vast waters of the world.

He began to understand how great and varied was Mettan'okit, our sacred mother, and that she had more children than he would ever meet. It was then that his idea came to him. He would listen to Mother Earth more carefully, listen and feel with more than just his ears and his feet.

He dug a deep hole on top of that hill, deep enough for him to stand in. When he was standing in it he filled with the dirt he had dug, covering himself with soil right up to his neck. In that way, he said, he could feel the embrace of the earth and receive her teachings directly through his whole being.

He felt like a plant with deep roots. The flowering of his face was visited by sun and wind and rain. The little ants passed over and around him on their busy rounds. He talked to them and praised their industry, and he spoke to the mosquitoes and greenhead flies visiting his face so that they did not sting him. His hair blew like the grass, and the smells and sounds of all the creatures filled him. He looked upon the sun rising from beyond the sea, watched the running clouds, and studied the wheeling patterns of the stars.

He lost consciousness of the passing time. But he heard other songs than those of the birds. He heard the songs and the stories of the times of the Old Ones and the instructions given by first-teacher Maushop.

There in the body of Mettan'okit, he saw that, even as he lay in the her embrace, so was he cradled ever by Pompaugusset, our Grandmother Ocean, and that they moved through a circle that contained Grandmother Moon, Grandfather Sun, and all the distant nations of stars. He saw that they and he were sacred, all part of one beautiful, vast, and mysterious Creation. He saw that all of it was holy.

After several days and nights, he knew not how many, he could feel Mettan'okit instructing him to return to his own land and his people. Weetucks understood that he was to tell the story of his journey to all who would listen. To teach the ways of Mettan'okit, the unity and sacredness of all things, and the instructions given the people by first-teacher Maushop, which they had forgotten. He felt there was more learning to come, and another important message to reveal, concerning his dream of the threat to the forest and all her creatures, including his people.

Weetucks then began slowly to move the loose soil and dig himself out from his hole. He had had nothing to eat, only one night's rain to drink, and he was very weak, but he managed to come out and walk all the way back to the village before he collapsed.

6. The Teachings of Weetucks

And now the village began to take pride in Weetucks. The story of his quest and his ordeal traveled quickly among the neighboring villages of the Pokonoket, those who settled the forests, the lake and river and salt-water bay shores. To all those bands that also inhabited the great cape and the islands. To their neighbors north, west and south called Wampanoag, People of the First Light, those who first see the sun rise from the sea. All the Children of the Morning Light, facing the dawn.

All the people of the village came to see this twelve year-old who had power, who had had visions and dreams, who had become a man of power and vision, a powwauh. Quickly there were too many for the little wetu where he lay, and every day they carried him outside to speak to the people. This was an unusual thing, something to learn about, to ponder and understand, a gift to the people, which they must give to their children, and they were very proud of their new young powwauh. Soon the village was full of visitors from other bands who came and sat quietly and listened patiently all day to the teachings of this unusual young man.

They did not only sit, however. He taught them ceremonies they had forgotten, thanksgiving ceremonies, honoring ceremonies, healing ceremonies. He taught them how to build and perform the pesuponk, the purification lodge and its ceremony. He had them rebuild the round house, the great lodge where all community could gather for ceremonies and dances.

Weetucks taught them songs and dances he had heard and seen in his dreams and visions. Most of these were ancient and the people had lost them, but some were new. And he told old stories they had forgotten. Stories about the morning of the world, when the stars and the earth were made. About Maushop and the first creatures, the animal people and the human people, who lived together in harmony and spoke the same language. Stories of the times of the ancient ones, when there was magic everywhere, and many were wizards of power, when there were giants in the hills, and the little people, the pugwudgies, living in a land where it was always summer, who would sometimes visit and play tricks. He told stories of the sky beings, the sea beings, and the beings under the earth.

Now Weetucks was honored in his own village. The people were proud of the special boy teacher who had come to them, and so also his mother was at last accepted and respected as a wise woman who had helped all this come to pass.

But the boy was not yet satisfied. It seemed to him that there was more to the work he had come to do, and he fasted and prayed to be shown what he must do. Somehow he understood it must involve the warning the wolf had brought him many years before.

Then Weetucks had another important dream. In this dream he was visited by two spirit beings from the Land of Souls beyond the sky. They told him that they had come to take his mother back to the Land of Souls, but also they had a prophecy to tell him.

The spirit beings told him that the knowledge he had received was part of the original instructions given by the Creator to the human people in the morning of the world. They spoke of a world in harmony, of life in balance. It was important for all creatures to follow their original instructions, but most important for the human people to understand and follow them. Because the other peoples, the plant people, animal people, bird people, insect people and all the others knew only their instructions and would follow them.

It was only the human people, given the sacred power of creativity, which means choice, who could choose to disregard the instructions. Only the human people could upset the balance of life, disturb the harmony, and visit destruction upon this world.

The spirit beings told that even now, in some parts of the earth, beyond the sea to the east there were human people who no longer followed the original instructions of harmony and balance. These people had abandoned the ways of respect and love. Driven by greed, these people were visiting violence and destruction upon the earth. Their history, for all time, would be one of pillage and conquest.

The messengers of his dream told Weetucks that those nations following paths of greed and violence would one day reach the shores of the Morning Light. The messengers said that at first the ways of these people would seem attractive and good. They would have better weapons and tools, and they would think the ways of the original people were inferior. Many would decide to follow this new path, since the invaders would seem so powerful.

For a while, the spirit beings told him, it would seem that these people were all-powerful, and that their way was inevitable. It would seem to be progress, the way of the future. But soon it would be seen that these new ways were not good. Eventually they would be found to be disastrous, destroying the earth, and our relatives of the plant and animal worlds, destroying people in violence and terrible loneliness, as people would be slowly separated from each other, from the earth mother and all her children.

In his dream Weetucks then saw his beloved forest in all its quiet majesty. Then the messengers showed him what was to come. He watched the tops of the trees begin to dry and the leaves turn black. The blackness spread downward, branches began to break, and then the trees began to topple over. The color went out of brushes and grass and every growing thing withered and fell and began to rot. With nothing to eat the little animals starved and the animals which fed upon them began to die too. The sun was hidden by a thick brown cloud, darkness remained a long time on the remains of the decaying earth.

The moon rose again and again over the silent world, finding no life anywhere. Lonely winds crossed the barren wastes, and the seas stroked the empty shores. But a song came from the sky, drawing the rain down to cleanse the earth. The song told of greenness and sweetness, a dream of beauty returning, and the stars twinkled in happiness to think it could be so.

Weetucks woke from his dream very troubled, and went quickly to where his mother slept. He could not wake her and he knew she was no longer there but had left her body behind, like an old dress. He understood then that her soul had left with the two spirit messengers on the star path that leads to the land of souls. Sadly he went into the forest to feel his feelings and think his thoughts.

Weetucks wept because his mother was gone. He was not alone. Some of the little animals and birds, feeling his grief, came out to sit quietly with him. Now he knew that his dream had been a true one, and that all his friends in the green world must one day face the destruction he had seen. He felt that now he needed to warn the people, yet somehow still give them hope.

Weetucks said farewell to his mother in the way that had been taught him by the spirits. He sat by the body that had clothed her spirit and sang songs with his rattle. This was to keep her soul company on her journey. He did this for four days, the time it was told that it would take for her to reach the Land of Souls. Then in the pesuponk, Weetucks prepared and purified the clothing of flesh his mother had worn in the old way, with smoke and, wrapping it in sacred birch bark, buried it in the bosom of Metta-n'okit. One more song he sang there, that their ancestors would remember and welcome his mother into the Land of Souls.

7. Weetuck's Warning

After that he went to the village and told the people he would have a ceremony by the river, near the place where he had entered the water seeking a vision. He told them to prepare a circular arbor there, and invite the people from other villages of the Pokonoket, and he would tell them of a prophecy that had been revealed to him.

When the three days had passed many people gathered there on the bank of Titicut, more people that had come together at any other time, for they were curious about the prophecy that had been shown to this twelve year old powwauh. They came from many bands, from the Assonet and the Pocasset, from the Assawompset and Nemasket, from Acushnet and Sakonnet, the Cohannet, Mettapoisett, from Montaup and from other villages even farther away.

Weetucks led the people down to the riverbank and showed them a large rock, almost as tall as he was, and twice as long. On the smooth southern face of this rock he had made carvings. At the edge of this face closest to the west he had carved a large figure, which he told them represented Kiehtan, the Creator. Next to that was a smaller figure which Weetucks said represented Kiehtan's helper, first-teacher Maushop. Across the center of the rock he had carved many fantastic shapes, animals and birds and fish and plants that were known to no one. This, he said, represented the vast unknown variety of beings in the Creation. At the eastern edge there were two human beings standing together. The first was looking back towards the Creator and Maushop and the marvelous figures of Creation. But the other was looking away, looking off the rock towards something beyond, towards the east. And over the head of this last person was carved a lightning bolt, pointing down right above him, pointing down to the top of his head.

Weetucks then explained the meaning of his carving. He told them of the new way that would come to them from the east, from beyond where the sun rises. He told them that they would follow different ways, and that the Children of the Morning Light would be tempted to follow these new ways, for they would seem attractive and good. People would actually begin to learn the new ways and forsake the old ways. But eventually it would be seen that these ways were destructive, that because of them the forest and the creatures of the forest, including the human people, would begin to be destroyed. That was what was meant by the lightning bolt above the head of the outer figure on the rock.

But those who continued to follow in a sacred path, the way of the Creator, and also those who saw their mistake in time and turned around to find Creation's' way again, these would survive to help heal the earth and restore the balance of life.

Weetucks said he had not been shown when this would happen. It might not be in their lifetime, so they must tell the story of the prophecy to their children, and tell them to tell their children and warn all the coming generations. Thus had he carved the vision upon this rock, to remind them and all the unborn to come of this danger.

Then Weetucks told the people it was time for him to leave. He must warn the other nations, he said, and spread the story of the prophecy among all the peoples of Turtle Island. Now should they feast and sing and dance and be glad for the goodness of life, but keep this message close to their hearts and always follow the sacred path, the way of the Creator.

And so saying, Weetucks turned from them, stepped upon the waters and walked across the top of the widening river towards the setting sun and was seen no more.

8. Epilogue ~ The Prophecy Rock

"And now," said the old storyteller, "shall we go see the rock?"

"Is this the same rock? Weetucks' rock?"

"Come and see what you think."

They entered the little stone house. On the walls were diagrams and drawings people had made of the rock and its carvings over the years. Some were over two hundred years old. Each one was different, as each person saw and drew the markings differently. Placards discussed the drawings, with theories as to who made the carvings, English, Irish, Portuguese, and many others. The story of Weetucks was not mentioned anywhere.

In the back the room was dark. The rock was encased entirely in glass, to prevent touching that might further erode the carvings. Lights across the bottom of the case threw the carvings into relief, but even so they were no longer clear enough to perceive whole images and patterns.

"How do you know this is Weetucks' rock? You can't see anything." One of the boys said.

"Look at the drawings," a girl said.

"They're none of them the same," said another," How can you know which is right?"

"I guess they are none of them right. Or all partly right."

"Look, you can see it if you study them," the older boy said, "See, there is the Creator, and there's Maushop, and all the fantastic beings of Creation, and over there are the human beings."

"Yes! There's the lightning bolt on this drawing - see it? Right over the head of the one looking away."

"Why isn't Weetucks mentioned anywhere?"

"Only a few people know that whole story. My grandfather told it to me when I was a boy, and he brought me here to see the rock. They had not sheltered it, and, as you see, the carvings were nearly gone, but he said they had been clearer when his father had shown it to him as a boy."

On the way back to the reservation the young people were quiet. Each was thinking his own thoughts. After they parked the van they saw that the older people had left the ceremonial grounds and were getting ready for a feast.

"Before we eat, could we go back to the arbor and have a ceremony of our own?" The older boy said.

"Would you show us, Grandfather? Would you lead us?"

"Let's go."

10. Epilogue ~

In a few minutes the young people stood within the ceremonial arbor, around the sacred fire, which the fire keeper had stirred with new wood for them. They had entered through the proper gates and now held hands in a circle, the girls in the south and the boys in the north.

"We have already begun our ceremonies at the river," the storyteller told them, "we have smudged ourselves with sweet grass and said our opening prayer. We have remembered the story of Weetucks, and we have paid our respects to the prophecy rock. Now we will pass the talking stick so that each of you may speak your mind and heart without interruption. Each one of you is unique and different. There has never been anyone like you before, and there never will be again. You each have been given special gifts with the gift of life. You were sent here by Creation to share those gifts, among which are the special ways you think and feel. To speak in the circle is part of your give-away to all of us. We need to hear and know what each one has to share.

"As you know, the circle is a great gift, part of our original instructions, and the instruction that is most essential to the circle, and to the talking stick, is respect. Here we respect each other, regardless of age or any other difference, and we respect the holder of the stick and give all our attention to that speaker. When you have the stick, respect for the listeners demands only your complete honesty, because we haven't time for anything else. Now I'm going to pass the stick, sun wise around the circle, to my left."

The oldest boy was the first to take the stick. He looked at it a moment, touching the wood, the carved head of a wolf, and the adornments of feathers, rabbit fur, and beads of black, white, red, and yellow, the sacred colors of the four directions.

"I want to thank the Creator for my life," he said, then looked at the storyteller, who nodded approval that the boy had remembered the proper way to begin. "And for the lives of my family," he went on, "and my elders, and my nation. And for bringing us together on this good day." He stopped and thought another moment. "Now that I am holding this talking stick and standing in this circle, I feel different. It is strange. New to me. But good. I feel different about the ceremony. I don't know what to say, except that speaking, and being heard, uh, well, it makes it feel like my ceremony, like our ceremony, and that feels good. Ho!" He passed the stick on.

The other boys used the same form they had heard the older boy use, thanking Creator for their lives, their families and elders, and for the circle. Most said they really didn't have much to say, but they were happy to be there and to hold the stick and feel that this was their ceremony.

"I guess I'm thinking about Weetucks," one said, "Does anyone know what happened to him, Grandfather?"

"Not exactly," the storyteller answered, "but I have traveled all over North America, and many people have tales of strange and wonderful messengers coming to them with stories and prophecies, teaching sacred ways. Maybe these visions happened to many people, but it could be that Weetucks also traveled far and visited these nations."

"He was younger than I am when he left. I wonder how he got to know so much," the boy said.

"That's because he lived in the woods and you live in a computer game," said a girl who sat next to him.

"Now remember to respect the stick - it's his turn to talk now."

"Okay, you want to talk, I'm finished - Ho!" The boy passed the stick on to the girl.

"I just wonder what that story really means to us now. We can't live in the woods anymore." She passed the stick on.

"If we could, would we?" The next girl wondered, "Would we know how? Would we want to? Are we too caught up in cars and washing machines and TV's? When we get out of school we'll have to get a job to pay rent. There's no way to live in the old ways today."

Melissa, the oldest girl had the stick now. She held it and looked at it and thought a while before she spoke.

"My greetings and thanksgivings to the Creator and all my relations everywhere," she began, "and to you, Grandfather, for that story. You told it to us for a reason. We are like the human being on the rock with the lightning over his head, the one who has gone on this new path which the Europeans brought to this land. And now we can see that this way is destroying us."

She stopped to see how the others were taking this. Some seemed puzzled, but they were all listening intently.

"We are confused." Melissa went on, "We have these toys now, these cars and computers and TV's. We also have poverty and homelessness, alcohol and drugs, and our families are torn apart. Young people our age are getting pregnant, getting AIDS, becoming violent, going to prison, and committing suicide. I mean, what's up with the world anyway? Look in the newspapers, all it is there is violence, war, the forests destroyed, the waters poisoned, the earth and air polluted. Am I right, or what?"

The others were nodding now. Melissa was speaking thoughts they had never shared with an adult before.

She looked around again. All eyes were on her. Many were nodding in agreement or encouragement. She looked at the ground, to gather her thoughts. Then she spoke more slowly.

"I don't know if we can live in the old ways anymore, but I know these new ways are destroying us, just as Weetucks said they would. And even if we stopped killing ourselves and the forests right now, what kind of life have we? There is so little love, so little joy. Everyone is searching for something better. We young people need something better to look forward to. But the culture can't give it to us.

"It teaches us that happiness is in competition, in personal glory, beating the others, in power and fame and wealth. We are measured by how big a job we have, how much money we make, and how much stuff we can buy, buy, buy! We are not taught joy in ourselves, in nature, in helping others, in families and communities, in little children and old people. When we want to do something we don't go to the forest we go to the mall.

"So if the story of Weetucks is true - " here she looked questioningly at the storyteller, who nodded to confirm the tale, "then the teachings of Maushop and Weetucks helped the people before. Perhaps that is why some of our old people have been trying to discover the old ways again. They have built this arbor and sacred fire circle here in the forest, and they come together for ceremonies, not all, but some, and more every year. They want the circle to grow and be strong again. They want our families and communities to come and grow together.

"We young people do not understand. We are caught up in the new ways, the electronic toys and games, the glamour of the latest fads and fashions. It's boring for us to sit around and listen to a lot of adults' talk we can't relate to. But today we all listened to Grandfather, and it seems that old story was important to each of us. Maybe this could be a beginning of something for us. Look at us now."

She paused. The young people looked at each other around the circle. Some smiled, some looked serious, but there was a new intensity in every eye, a new energy moving among them. They could all feel it.

"Something has happened since we made a circle here. Can't you feel this power? We are thinking together, listening more and coming closer to each other. Holding the talking stick has stirred truth and caring in each of us. This is our circle now. It feels important. Perhaps here we can find our own way, our own path back to the Creator's way and the original instructions. HO!"

The talking stick had come full circle, back to the Old Storyteller. He smiled at the young people, and they all smiled back.

"I am proud of you all, my Grandchildren," he said at last. "You are truly Children of the First Light. The spirits of these woods are watching now. They have seen our ancestors gather in circles about a sacred fire and seek the true path of the Original Instructions of the Creator. In other places the forests and these ways are disappearing, so these spirits must feel good that you are here at last, remembering the teachings of Maushop and Weetucks.

"The ways of our ancestors are in your hands. If you carry them well, if you walk in a sacred manner through this forest and this life, making every step upon Our Sacred Mother the Earth a prayer of thanksgiving, you will make a path that is safe for seven generations to follow. It is important that we carry these instructions to the unborn, so that our people will survive as they have, without disturbing the balance and the harmony of Creation. Perhaps there will be a new morning after all, a green forest world and a good life for the People of the Dawn.'"

When they left the forest there was a secret lightness in their hearts. They looked forward to coming back. It was truly their forest now.

WOLF DREAMER

So you want another story? All right, get comfortable and listen. Let's see. We have to find just the right story for you and for this moment. What's that? Oh, you want a scary story. Heh, I wonder what it is about camping out in the woods everyone always asks for scary stories. Something to do with the dark all around closing us into our puny little fire, and all the night noises, the threat of the unknown, of strange things that haunt our nightmares. Puts us in the mood to get scared of our wits.

Now what's going on, eh? Come on, don't say "nothing" because I've been right here watching and listening when you didn't notice me. Maybe you need to hear one of the old stories about that Annungitee who comes to carry off bad boys. Okay, I know you are good boys, all of you. So why are you picking on this fellow? Just because he's a shorty and smaller than the rest of you? What? You say he's a liar? Aha, well....

What about the stories I tell? Are the stories true?

That's the question I get more than any other when I tell the legends of our people. Especially monster stories. Maybe I'm a liar too, only you are all too respectful to say it. Because the stories are full of fantastic things you've never seen or heard. Animals that talk, that change shape, magic powers, sorcerers, witches, monsters, giants, little people, ghosts, demons.

Well... these are only facts. Externals. Truth is internal, not on the surface, but imbedded in the spirit. Artists, storytellers, are not interested in the facts, they are only interested in the truth. The surface of life as we see it all about us is very misleading. Reality is incredibly mysterious. The real monsters lie inside us, and our fears are real enough. The only way we can hope to pursue truth is on an inward journey, don't you see, a journey that turns deliberately from appearances into mystery. Do you all understand what I mean? Hmmm....well.

What's out there, in the dark? You don't really know, do you? What you see and hear and feel can always fool you. What's going on out there? It's what's going on inside you right now. Would you go out there now, all alone by yourself, in those dark woods? Well.

Did you ever hear the story about Penatook, the Wolf Dreamer? No?

Well, you see, that Penatook, he was a shorty too. But it turned out he had a special power. You know, we come in all sizes - human beings. And we're all different. We all have been given different gifts, different powers. You each have one, just yours. There was never anyone like you before, and there never will be again in all this world. So you better find your power, learn about your gift so you can give it away, give it back to Creation and to your people, like Penatook.

All right, this is the time for that story. What happened to him out here one night, in these very woods, just across the next valley, a long time ago, became a legend of our people. Listen.

27

At that time there was a boy among our people called Penatook. Know what that means? Little Wolf. And he was little for his age, like this boy here, small, dark, slight, maybe even skinny. And the other boys used to kid him about never making it as a hunter because he wasn't as strong as they and couldn't run so fast or throw a spear or shoot arrows so well. They'd say things like, "Don't get caught in a rabbit trap." They weren't mean, just having fun like you fellows. But Penatook didn't like it. And that's why he started to lie. His friends teased him about being small, so he made up stories about adventures he had in the woods in which he was always a brave hero, saving the village from monsters and demons and terrible things. Of course everyone just laughed at him.

When his uncle saw that, he took pity on Penatook and decided to teach them all a lesson. He took all the boys to camp out in the woods, just the way I am taking all of you. And after dinner they all lay around the fire in their blankets just as we are now, and Penatook's uncle told them stories, just like I'm doing now. He told them the story about the Great Head that has no body and moves about on the power of his long hair, whose magic is so strong that whatever he sees dies from his look. And about Pitcher the Witch that has all these mean nasty black cats that do whatever she says. And he told about another witch, Kitchi-M'teolin, who lives in a cave up north, who has a heart of ice and can be a man or woman as he chooses and make herself any size, and if you hear his singing you come under her spell and have to go there. His cave is lined with the bones of those who listened to her song.

He told them stories about Annungitee, Two Faced, an ugly spirit with huge ears that hears everything and who makes strange noises when he comes to carry off boys who are bad-acting. Noises like owls, or whispering, or bells, or buffalo snorting. Listen! What do you hear right now?

Well...then he spoke about the Windigo who live under the earth who can be friendly or they can just eat your soul. About the terrible Chenoo, devil man-beasts that come from the frozen north, so tall their heads are above the clouds, who rip up forests and crush rocks to powder. Their scream is fatal to all who hear it, and the food they love best is your liver.

And he told about a great black wolf that was once a man, and he can change back to a man and be among you and you'd never know he's really a wolf, and who comes to camps like this while you are all asleep, and he can tear your throat out so fast you can't cry out, and then he drags you off to his lair and his sharp-toothed little cubs chew on you while you are still alive.

Well, you see, he got all those boys pretty scared. Before he finished they weren't even sure that the uncle wasn't a wolf-man, and they really didn't want to go to sleep. Especially when he told them whatever you dream about that's what you're going to call to yourself.

So they got talking about dreams, and Penatook, he told them about a dream he kept having and what did it mean. It was about a wolf. That wolf's head just kept popping up in his dreams, looking at him. Sometimes it was only the wolf's eyes that appeared. What kind of eyes, I mean what was their expression, what did they want to say to you? the uncle wanted to know. Well, Penatook thought the eyes were questioning him, but he didn't understand the question, so he couldn't answer.

Yes, the uncle told him, dreams are important and to dream of a wolf is very good. You understand, for our people a wolf is not scary. He is not an enemy, he is our teacher. We are the People of the Dawn, but we are also often called the People of the Wolf. It was the wolf who first told that a tribe is a family and taught us how to be a family. He taught us about loyalty and devotion to each other and to the pack, about cooperating as we hunt together, about honoring the elders and caring for the little ones. In a wolf family the male and the female are equal. As in our people, either one can be the chief, and if one dies the other will go on caring for the cubs.

The next time you dream of the wolf, the uncle told Penatook, ask him what instructions or what request he has. If the wolf were to give him a good vision it would be important. Then he could be called Wolf Dreamer.

But when they were getting ready to sleep the other boys teased Penatook about his dreaming. They thought it was just another lie he made up to make himself look powerful. Perhaps in the dark he may have wept very quietly, and it was with bitterness that Penatook finally slept. In his dream the wolf's eyes came to him again, and this time they seemed to be pleading, to be asking for help. And at the same time he heard the wolf's voice for the first time, not a howl, but a whine of a creature in pain.

Penatook woke. It was still the blackest part of night, and he could hear the breathing of the others asleep around him. Then he heard that whine again. It was not in his dreams this time, but it was far off in the dark forest. Remembering the wolf's pleading eyes, Penatook rose quietly, put on his moccasins, and started out in the direction of the wolf's whining call.

It was difficult moving through that forest in the dark. He couldn't see what was under his feet and often stumbled on stones or holes or tripped on branches and bumped into trees. Leaves and twigs brushed and scratched his face. Sometimes the ground went up hill, sometimes it dipped down. Always he followed the persistent whine of the wolf as it got louder and louder, and slowly he drew closer until he seemed to come out into a clearing and the whining stopped.

He stared into the dark in silence. All he could feel was his heart pounding inside him. All he could hear was the sound of his own breath panting in short huffs.

Then for a moment the pounding of his heart stopped because suddenly he heard the sound of another breath breathing together with his own! He held his breath then, there with nothing but blackness ahead, and listened to the breathing of some other creature. The breathing seemed to come from all around and filled him with horror. Then it stopped and all he could hear was the wind, which was suddenly coming strong ahead of him. Slowly, carefully, he began to step across that black empty place that seemed to be a clearing. The wind kept getting stronger ahead of him, blowing in his face.

All at once his foot slipped and he started to fall backward. At the same time he thought he heard a little "yip" - not quite a bark- behind him, the wind came up fiercely from ahead and below him and he sat down hard. His feet being lower than his seat, he began to feel around him in the dark. It seemed he had fallen right at the edge of a precipice, and the way the wind was whipping up from below it was perhaps quite a deep drop before him. Now he was glad he had fallen backward and not forward. He could have been dead or all smashed up at the bottom of a cliff. Well, now that he thought of it, there had been a feeling almost of someone pushing him back. He thought it was the wind - but was it?

One thing was certain. He was not going to move again until first light. He was sitting now and safe and he should leave it at that. He was exhausted from scrambling through the woods. His legs were bruised and his face was scratched. But he was alive. And safe.

Or was he? There at the edge of a precipice, facing a black wind from unknown regions, the images of the stories his uncle told began to come to him. Those demon Pook-jin-skwess seemed to be crawling up the face of the cliff towards him, clawing at his feet. The awful Kewahq was creeping up on him from behind, the fearful Hobbomocko was laughing, ready to pounce as soon as he moved, wicked Cheepii had turned into his serpent self and was crawling towards him over the ground, and the vile and ghoulish Chenoo were riding out there on the ghastly winds from the north, coming ever closer, smacking their lips at the thought of gnawing at his liver and nibbling on his brains.

Well, you can see that to Penatook it seemed that all that murky, eerie night was filled with unseen demons and ghosts wailing and howling in the wind. In dire terror he hunched himself up, bringing his knees to his chin, clasping them together in his arms and making himself just as small as he could. The wind got stronger and colder. His teeth were chattering. His skin was prickling and growing numb. Whatever was out there was coming closer, and now it seemed he could hear a faint whispering, as of voices in the wind, now growing louder in his ears.

"YOU! Yoooou! Nosey, Ssssorry, Sssscrimpy, Falssssse!" they hissed, "You dare to come here in our place in our night? You will be sorry! We are coming to devour you. First your skin, then your blood, and your entrails, and last of all," this now with a screech, "YOUR SOUL!" Then came a wild scream, the force of which almost felled him, and the cold sensation of wind now seemed to be full of teeth and claws snatching at him everywhere, so that with tears of panic pouring down his face he cried out against the wind.

"Oh, Grandfather Wolf, help me! Save me!" And now the voices got louder than ever and the baleful clutching at him stronger. Penatook wanted to cry out again, but his voice was choked with fright. He kept his eyes and mouth shut tight and prayed in his mind and with all his soul to Grandfather Wolf. Behind his close eyelids two red dots appeared and grew into ovals and grew further into eyes, wolf's eyes, the color of blood, the color of fire.

Under the shrieks of wind he heard a low growl, and the scratching of invisible claws and fangs abruptly ceased. The wind wailed louder, and something seemed to be roaring in the wind, in protest. But the growl then became the long, eerie, blood-chilling howl of a wolf that hushed every sound and stilled the wind and echoed across the distant hills of night.

Silence then. Not a breath of wind. The cold receded and the darkness warmed. Exhausted, tears dried on his face, Penatook slept.

He woke to the sound of birds singing. It was still dark in the woods, but the light had begun to fill the sky behind the hills which he saw ahead of him, across a steep valley. He could see now that he was indeed at the crest of a tall hill, poised at the edge of a cliff so steep and deep he could not see the bottom. Carefully he rose and withdrew from the abyss. As the light began dimly to filter into the forest he slowly retraced his steps, seeking a trail. He didn't know where he had gotten to in the night. He recognized nothing and felt utterly lost.

By a creek bottom he suddenly heard again the whimpering whine that had drawn him from his blankets in the night. Again he felt the same calling, the need to follow the cry to its source. Guided by the direction of the keening he continued and presently discovered a path, down which the sound beckoned him. Half hidden beneath a bush beside an open place in the forest he discovered the sender of the call. Lying there regarding him with piteous eyes a female wolf was sobbing through her open mouth. She seemed to be pleading with him, and very cautiously he came closer. She continued to watch him and whine, and he continued to move nearer until at last she raised her open mouth to him and he saw blood encircling her teeth. Murmuring affectionately to her, Penatook reached out and touched her mane, stroked the top of her head. She lay perfectly still for his advances, so he was emboldened to grasp her muzzle very gently and peer into her mouth. After some searching he could see a sizable splinter of wood that was imbedded deep inside. Carefully, carefully he reached his fingers into her mouth and grasped the end of the splinter firmly.

"Hold on, Mother Wolf, I'm going to pull that out now and it may hurt, so don't bite me!"

With that he jerked the splinter, and though it resisted, he pulled stoutly so that it relinquished its hold and came out in a gush of sudden warm blood. The wolf stood, coughed, let the blood flow from her mouth, then rubbed her head against the boy's leg in gratitude. Penatook knelt and put his arms about the animal and buried his face in her fur.

"Thank you for saving me last night." He held her then for a long time and she stood patiently to let him, his first real friend. Finally he stood and wiped his eyes, for he had been crying just a little, out of new found joy and love.

"But I don't know which way I must go now. I'm afraid I have gotten pretty lost." As soon as he said this, the wolf trotted off down the path, then stopped and looked back, waiting. The boy understood she meant him to follow, which he did, and in a short time she had returned him to the outer circle of his own village. He started to go in, but the wolf had stopped and was sitting, watching him.

"Can't you come too? I want you to stay with me forever!" But the wolf's answer was to get up and turn and run back down the path into the woods.

The first thing Penatook did when he got home was to sleep, through the day and through the night, and the next morning he was rested and strong. The other young people came to ask about his night alone in the forest, but he did not feel like talking about it. For the first time he did not want to boast or make up a story about his heroism. He had known great terror and he had survived and was changed. The change made him just a bit proud, but also quite humble, and rather quiet inside. He told no one, not even his uncle, about his encounter with the wolf. He knew now that he was a wolf dreamer, but he did not know yet what that meant.

The talk in the village just then was all about the hunt, which was very poor just then. The best scouts had found no tracks and the best hunters came home empty-handed. Penatook felt a new concern for his people now. He had the heart of a wolf, with all its loyalty and devotion to the pack. Knowing that the wolf was his helper, he prayed that night.

"Grandmother and Grandfather Wolf, our people are hungry and starving. It seems there are no more deer or moose or elk or even bears in our lands. Perhaps we shall have to leave this home where our ancestors are buried, but even that will be hard when there is no food and the people are so weak."

Penatook fell asleep thinking about his wolf protector. And so, that wolf came again in his dream that night. He saw himself travelling about in barren lands with a pack of wolves led by that Grandmother Wolf he had helped. She taught him how to track and hunt with the pack, riding on her back, and she taught him the song the wolves sing to each other, to the hills, and to the moon.

When he woke in the early morning before dawn he could still hear that song echoing from his dreams. Then it became clearer and more near and he realized it was not in his dream now but coming from somewhere just outside the village. He rose and went outside. The early mist was so strong he could barely make out the trees at the edge of the clearing. He could see that the early hunting party had left some time ago, and the dogs were gone with them. Then he heard the wolf howl again, low, not loud, but not far away. He went down the path towards the sound.

When he came to the clearing at the outer circle he saw her. She was sitting at the other end of the clearing just under the trees. Behind her he could barely make out movement in the mist, the forms of other wolves in the pack moving back and forth behind her. Grandmother Wolf sat still, watching him with friendly eyes. When he came closer he saw that she was sitting behind the carcass of a freshly killed deer. Before he got to where she was she rose, gave him a little nod, and trotted off into the murky forest with the rest of her pack.

That night everyone in the village was able to partake of venison stew. The people thought it a great wonder that little Penatook, smallest of the young people, had been the one to bring them meat when their best hunters could not. Not only that, but this former liar told no story about the kill to make himself appear great. There were many who thought he must have come across a deer who had died from an accident.

But the next morning when he rose he heard the low howl again, and once more found an animal, this time a moose, lying just outside the village. The pack waited just long enough to be sure that he saw the moose before they again trotted off into the mysterious depths of the forest. This moose gave meat to all in a great feast. Strength and hope were returning to the people. Now they knew there was something special happening, and that it had to do with Penatook. When they asked him he told them that it was his friends the wolves. And his uncle told everyone about Penatook's dream, so they saw that the wolves had adopted him, and by extension, their whole village.

Every morning of his life from that time on the wolves came and presented him with a deer, a moose, an elk, or some other large animal that the pack had driven to the village and killed. The people never had to be hungry again, and they were very grateful, calling themselves the Wolf People, and Penatook taught them the song he had learned in his dream, the Song of the Wolf. Ever since then, from that time to this, the people told their children and passed down to all generations to come the legend of Penatook, the Wolf Dreamer.

WEQUASH'S WORLD

Wequash was confused.

She drew back the moose-robe door and peered out of her family's wetu at the other winter longhouses of her village. Hoping that Auntie might be in sight. There was little movement. The bare branches of the trees moved in a brisk breeze. A few of the village dogs looping about sniffing each other and the tracks in the dirty old snow. But there was no human being anywhere. It was people she needed to talk to, grown people who had seen and heard more of the mysteries that lay beyond her village. In her own wetu was only her grandmother's mother, watching the center fire. Wequash would not ask her questions because she could never understand the old woman's toothless speech.

Her friend Mequin had just told her some very unsettling things. Mequin's brother had said there were other beings in the world, not like the animals, but not like the people either. Beings that stood on two legs and made sounds that sounded like talking but didn't make any sense. Mequin didn't believe him, of course. Chepacket was always trying to fool her, telling her whoppers and insisting they were true, and when Mequin began to believe he would laugh at her. She refused to be fooled by him again.

Wequash didn't know what to believe. Giant two-leggeds? That looked almost like human beings but bigger and hairier and smellier? She knew everyone in her village, of course. And she understood that there were a few other people in the world, in places beyond her village. Her two uncles and a cousin had married women from other villages and gone to live there. And she had gone with her aunt to visit the nearest village often. Her cousins there told her about other villages they had visited. And every one of the twelve summers of her life she had gone with her father and mother, her two little brothers and her auntie to live by the sea, where she met people from other tribes - Narragansett and Massachuset and Nipmuc. But they all looked and spoke like human beings.

How many people could there be in the world? How far does the world go? Is it possible there are many other villages, as many as there are stars in the sky? That there are lands beyond the shores of Pokonoket and many different and strange peoples? That's what Mequin said, but Wequash didn't believe it. How could that be, and how would Mequin's brother know? If that were true....

Suddenly the world, her world of familiar people and animals, of woods and paths and meadows and waterways, didn't seem safe and reliable any more. It was mysterious and unpredictable. How could Wequash know what was real and what was possible? She was confused and she didn't like these thoughts. In her family's wetu she felt secure and safe. All the long winter and spring they lived in this longhouse here in the village. Here there were three fires. Her mother and her auntie, the one with no children, kept one fire for her father and his children. Two other aunties with their husbands and children kept the fire on the other end. And the center fire was kept by her grandmother, the mother of her mother and her aunties, for her grandfather and her granny's mother, who was pretty old.

She had asked Mequin's brother, but Chepacket had not laughed at her. His eyes grew wider when he answered.

"I overheard some of the elders talking," he had said. "These creatures appeared in the north, coming by sea in big canoes with serpent heads and white wings. They were tall and bulky and covered with fur of different colors, yellow and white and red and brown, with furry faces and horns on their heads! They said there was a fight and the human beings lost and ran away." Chepacket could say no more. Always if he were making it up he would embroider with many more fantastic details. And Mequin's brother had not seemed so sure of himself and so dramatic as he usually did when he was story-telling. He seemed truly puzzled, perhaps even fearful.

Now Wequash was only waiting for her auntie. Auntie knew a lot, and she would answer her questions. She always did.

She looked down the length of the wetu now. It was warm and pleasant in the dim rosy glow of the three fires. The long straight ash trees that were dug deep in the earth and bent like bows into an arch made a vaulting frame covered with heavy elm bark. Covering the inside were many mats woven thick of birch bark, poplar and ash splints, which insulated walls and ceiling, except for the smoke holes over each fire. The fires were circled with rocks that could be arranged to hold pottery cooking jars over the hot coals, and tripods from which could be hung food for roasting.

Where was Auntie? Wequash hadn't seen her since just after first light, and now it was after mid-day. She sat on her bed, a frame raised the two hands above the cold ground, a heavy moose hide, sagging like a hammock, tied to the frame and supported by cross-strips of sinew and covered by her very soft elk blanket. Her grandfather had made that. She ran her hand over its smooth surface. Her grandfather could make elk hides softer than anybody. As she thought of that she looked over at her snowshoes propped against the edge of the bed. She should hang them up, she thought. Her grandfather had made those too. They were so fine, so many thongs tied in an intricate, complex design. More than just a simple crosshatch to keep you above the snow, these were creations of great beauty.

Her father and her uncles also made beautiful things. There was another question - people always say it's right to have humility, but was it wrong for her to be so proud of her whole family? Her eyes traveled down the length of the lodge noticing the spears and bows and shields hanging on all the walls, dyed blankets and robes, some made by her grandfather but mostly made by the women, as were the woven mats, the pottery, the baskets. The men had carved wooden utensils and animal figures Not every family's lodge was as full of so many handsome artifacts. How could she not be proud of all that?

Granny had returned from outside and was feeding her old mother a soup she had just taken from the central fire. Granny must be old too, Wequash thought, but she didn't look old, and she didn't act old. She was strong and quick, always busy, always active, from first light until everyone lay down at night. She looked more like an older sister than a mother to her daughters. She seemed always to know everything that was going on in the lodge, and in her daughters' families. She never criticized if she thought anything was done wrong, but if she had a chance she would quietly set it right for herself.

The old woman seemed, on the other hand, truly ancient. Perhaps because she had lost almost all her teeth and her face was sunken in on itself and heavily lined. Her gnarled hands shook too much to hold a soup ladle, so her daughter patiently and slowly brought it to her lips, smiling and talking to her softly in loving tones. A soft wave of loving feelings rushed on Wequash. What a nice woman Granny was! She treated all her grandchildren as if they were each special and wonderful. She listened with interest to them prattle on about anything at all and she never spoke harshly to anyone. If she wanted to correct one of them she would only say that their people had a different way of doing it, and to be fully grown human beings of her family and her village they needed to learn how to do it in this way.

Wequash went and squatted beside Granny and watched her feed her mother.

"Granny? Are there really giants?"

"I have heard stories of those great ones. Also of the little people."

"Yes, but are they real? Have you ever seen them? Has anyone in our village, anyone in your life, ever seen them? Big creatures that look like human beings but have yellow fur and horns on their heads, that make funny sounds and smell real bad?"

"Not me, anyway. Ask your father. He meets a lot of people and hears a lot of stories in his travels."

Wequash went back to her bed and sat. Her father was not so easy to talk to. Nor her mother either. They were good people, never raised their voices, went about their separate work quietly and efficiently. But they did not either of them talk too much to Wequash or her brothers. If the boys needed instruction the uncles would take them for a walk and talk to them. Of course her brothers never told her what the uncles said, but she noticed changes in how the boys did things after these walks.

It was her auntie that told her things mostly. She knew her aunt's name but only called her and thought of her as Auntie. Her mother's other sisters were Auntie Kria and Auntie Metta, but the one that shared their fire, the one with no man and no children of her own, she was just Auntie to Wequash. It was Auntie whom she needed to ask.

She had heard that Auntie had a husband and a baby once, but the husband had been lost in a storm at sea and the baby had gotten sick and died. Auntie had been alone ever since Wequash had known her. Wequash thought perhaps they were so close because Auntie's sisters all had husbands and children and she had no one. Since Wequash was the only girl at their fire it was natural for the two of them to become intimate. It was Auntie who taught her the things a girl should know, how to clean the fish, skin the animals the men brought in, to tan the hides and prepare thongs and sinew thread and cords, how to make robes, sew clothes, to make pots of clay and fire them, how to prepare and cook the meat, seafood, and corn, beans, squash, and wild herbs and roots, how to split splints and weave baskets and mats.

And when she didn't understand how something was done, or what something was for, or what was happening or going to happen, there was Auntie to turn to. Wequash couldn't ask others. She would be too embarrassed or ashamed. They might laugh at her for being so ignorant or foolish. Her mother and Granny were always so busy, she couldn't take up their time with a little girl's questions. Sometimes she used to ask her mother things, but if the answers were complicated and long her mother just told her to ask Auntie. And Auntie always took such time and care to explain everything and to be certain that Wequash understood. Her aunt made her feel that what Wequash asked was just the right question at that time and very important. She made Wequash feel smart instead of stupid for asking.

All the men of the lodge, Grandfather included, were out on a hunt. Game is scarce in winter, but snows had begun to melt and hungry animals were becoming bolder in scouring the muddy earth for food. Her brothers, two and three years younger, were out collecting fallen branches for firewood. Her mother and aunts must be visiting other families, she thought. Only Granny and her mother remained.

She needed Auntie. If anyone knew about these giants, Auntie would know. But Wequash had already looked in the other wetus in the village, and Auntie wasn't there. There was nothing to do; she had thought about it all she could.

She had just decided to get up and ask Granny if there was anything she could do for her when suddenly there was a flash of light as the bright day outside stabbed through the door. When the moose-robe door fell back and returned the lodge to its rosy shadows, there was Auntie tall and vibrant, flushed with brisk walking in the wind, standing beside her.

"Well, here you are, Wequash! Why are you sitting alone inside on this fine day?"

"I - I looked for you, but I couldn't find you."

"Yes, I went to the lake. The ice is all gone, the creek is really rushing with melted snow." She took off her fur cap, smoothed back a few wild strands of black hair and replaced the cap over them. "There are buds on the trees, more birds are around, and there's a feeling of spring everywhere. Come, see! Let's walk around."

Wequash was happy now and excited as she walked beside her aunt on a trail well worn in the snow. The fur on the inside of her coat was soft and friendly and she felt warm and good inside. Auntie was a head taller and walked with a long swift stride so Wequash had to skip quickly along to keep up. Soon they were standing together at the shore of the lake, silently watching little patches of ripples move slowly around on the surface.

"Auntie, are there giants?"

"You mean like in the stories of the old times, the great stone people that became mountains?"

"No. These are different. Mequin says that big two-leggeds with yellow fur and horns on their heads attacked some human beings. Somewhere up north. Her brother told her. I don't know where he got that from. Maybe he was just teasing - he does that."

"Well, Wequash, it just happens that I heard something myself. I don't know if it was giants or large human beings or some other kind of animal. A friend in Naumkeag has an uncle who lives with his Wabanaki wife up north. He is visiting there now, and it is from him that this story is being told."

"Tell it to me, please."

Auntie didn't speak for a few moments and seemed to be thinking as they watched a ripple move on the lake that might have been a fish or a turtle. When she turned to Wequash there was a gleam of excitement in her look.

"Better than that, let's go hear the story from the man himself. I didn't hear so much, and I don't know if it was told right. It's always best to talk to the man who has seen with his own eyes."

"Could we really do that? Is it far to Naumkeag?"

"A day and a half if we only stop for the night. We'll leave tomorrow morning. Go light, take only some parched corn, some pemmican and journey-cake. No snow-shoes, we'll keep to the trails, and no blankets, we'll stay with relatives in Shawmut."

Travel was fast. It had not snowed in a month and the trails were well worn. The spring-like weather continued, and sometimes they ran through the quiet woods for a while, feeling light of heart and exhilarated. It was more than just travel or adventure. As they moved beyond the woods and fields familiar to her, Wequash felt something opening in her, new vistas appearing to her, before her eyes and in her mind. The world was not the small place she had always known. There was more than she knew - and more than Auntie or perhaps anyone knew. Fear and curiosity and excitement stirred in her in equal measure.

At the home of a distant cousin in Shawmut they asked if anyone had heard about the giants, but the story was unknown there. Stimulated by the mystery now they lay down at dark. Wequash wanted to ask Auntie what she had heard from her

41

friend, but was so tired from the journey she was soon asleep and dreaming of being chased by tall hairy creatures that smelled bad. The next thing she knew Auntie was telling her to get up, and they rose before first light to continue on to Naumkeag.

They followed a river downstream towards the smell of salt breezes and found the village sheltered behind bluffs on a small peninsula thrust into the bay, which was sprinkled toward the sea with great rocks and small rocky islands. The village was larger than their own, but Auntie seemed to know just where her friend's lodge was, even though it had been many years since she had visited. As was the custom, Suttaquin, Auntie's friend, made them comfortable by the fire and gave them succotash from a large pot sitting in the coals. Suttaquin's husband, Namset, was out with her uncle, showing him the fish weirs and the nets they were preparing for the herring run that would soon begin. The hot corn and beans had pieces of dried and smoked venison and fish and chunks of raccoon fat in it. It tasted dusky and rich and was very satisfying. Wequash asked Suttaquin about the giants, but she said they must wait and hear the story right from her uncle.

After they ate, Suttaquin took them out to find Namset and her uncle. Many people of the village were out on this fine day working on their boats. There were quite a few dugouts, like the Mishawmuck of their own people, but there were also boats Wequash had never seen, canoes of birch bark and some small craft whose light frames were stretched over with animal skins of some kind. The breeze was light and the sea was quiet and many people had their boats in the water, trying them out after the long winter, looking for leaks. Some of the canoes were gathered a ways out, and the men in them were driving poles down to repair and complete weirs that had been battered by winter storms. Everywhere Wequash looked around that bay she saw rocks, and she wondered how they could find any place sandy enough to sink fish weirs in. At the shore where they went in summer it was all sand, the very few rocks all well known to the mariners.

Suttaquin's husband was discovered soon talking to a group of men about the nets, the canoes, and the weather, universal subjects for fishermen everywhere. Her uncle was joking and laughing with all of them as though he had lived there all his life, and had not married a Wabanaki girl more than twenty springs ago and been away to the north all that time. His name was Omogom, a funny name meaning "almost a fish". Wequash looked at him closely. He did not look like a fish. Stocky and thick, with a chest larger than his belly and shoulders wider than all the rest of him, he was not much taller than Wequash herself. His face was very brown and creased in a way that made you think he must laugh a great deal. He got his name, she found out later, because he seemed to always know where the tribes of fish gathered and moved.

Wequash was eager to hear the story of the giants, of course, but she had to practice patience. All her people learned this from childhood. It seemed the two

42

words Wequash and her brothers heard most in their lives were respect and patience. Respect everything, she heard it again and again when she was small. Respect the earth, respect the plant people, the animal people, the fish people, even the stone people. Respect the fire, the water, the tools, the weapons, the houses, the canoes. Respect the elders, the little ones, your family and your clan.

And when the elders talked - that's when you learned patience! Most of the elders didn't like to talk so much, just gave their greetings and their thanksgivings. But some of them could talk and talk for hours! Mostly men - when women talked it was because they had something to say, and then you better listen good! But a lot of the men just liked to hear the sound of their words.

When she was little she would just run off and play with the other little ones. But if you wanted people to know you were growing up, becoming an adult, then you had to sit quietly and at least pretend to listen. It was a time when you could think a lot of thoughts. At first she had tried hard to listen and really learn from the elders. And she did learn, from some. If she couldn't concentrate, she thought she must be too stupid, or too young, and she didn't want anyone to know that, so she looked as though she were listening intently. But quickly she found out that some men just spin out words like music, not meaning anything. Then her thoughts would drift away. Something someone said would send her mind on a long journey of wondering and imagining.

Now she sat in the wetu with Auntie, Namset and Suttaquin, listening to Omogom while they ate their dinner. But he did not talk about giants! She wanted so much to ask, but that would not be polite, so she listened and practiced her patience. Omogom talked about his family in the north, about his four children who were all older than Wequash. They were working on the nets and the canoes, but winter still set heavily in the northland, and Omogom was taking this time before spring to visit his old family at Naumkeag. Suttaquin, her brother and two sisters and a couple of cousins were all that were left there. The elders of the family had gone on their spirit journey, and several other men had married into other villages and moved away.

When the eating was done and everyone gathered around the fire, the men, after offering a little of the tobacco to the fire with a thanksgiving, filled their small stone pipes and smoked thoughtfully for a few minutes before Namset turned to Auntie.

"And what gives us the pleasure of this visit today, Nadtonkas?"

"I heard of your coming to Naumkeag and decided it would be a good time to visit my old friend Suttaquin and let my niece Wequash see a bit more of the world. We were both eager to meet and listen to you, as we have heard that you have wonderful tales of your travels in the northlands."

"It's good to have some new victims, I have already worn out everyone's ears here with my stories." He grinned broadly and his chest shook as though with laughter, but he made no sound.

"We always like to hear them again, Omogom," said Suttaquin.

"And what did you manage to hear so far away in your village?"

"Interesting stories travel faster and farther than anything else," Auntie said. "But sometimes they alter on the journey, so we have come to hear from the source."

"Which tale interested you the most?"

"We heard something about giants, or some kind of great furry creatures," said Wequash.

"Ah, of course, it must be that. I must tell you I am not truly the source. I was not there. But my wife's elder uncle told us from his own eyes what happened. It is a story that astonishes everyone who hears it. Indeed I have heard him tell it so often, that I think I can speak it just as he does."

"Please, oh, please, tell it to us now!" Wequash could not contain herself and almost jumped up and down as she sat, like a small child. Everyone laughed, and then grew quiet as Namset stirred the fire and put on more wood while Omogom waited for the pictures and the words to come together in his mind.

"Keeony, my wife's uncle, made a journey to visit a brother who lived with his wife's family far to the north. There they heard from travelers of strange beings traveling in huge canoes that had come down from even further north. These canoes had serpent's heads and tails, many very long paddles coming out of both sides, and a large wing of skin that hung from a tree in the middle and filled with wind that bore them along. The canoes carried many kinds of creatures never before seen, and Keeony and his friends decided to journey north to see them for themselves."

Omogom was silent again, staring into the play of the flames around the logs. Wequash and the others watched where he looked in the fire, as if to see what he saw there. When he spoke again it seemed almost as though he was taking them all along on that expedition to the north. In the pictures formed by his words in the shifting flames and coals Wequash lived the story just as he told it.

It had been in the autumn, he said, when his wife's people had first heard of these strange beings. Keeony had paddled northward with other men of his brother's village in nine skin canoes. At the estuary of a river which empties into a large sound they came upon two of these huge canoes tied to the shore and a number of strange square houses made of logs and earth had been built under the lee of cliffs behind. Suddenly there were a lot of great two-leggeds coming from the houses and from the woods and calling to each other. Some of these seemed not much larger than human beings, but most were a head or even two heads taller, very broad in shoulder and body, covered with fur of various colors. Most of them had much fur on their faces, but the smaller ones' faces were bare. The bare faces, arms and upper legs were mainly white or pink. Many wore breast coverings that shined like copper but were more yellow and carried axes, spears, and long knives, and most had caps of the same shiny stuff. They were truly beings of terrifying aspect.

Keeony and his friends waved their spears in sunwise circles to show they were peaceful, and the giants waved back. Our people then drew their canoes onto the shore, looking at the giants from a safe distance, and counciled about what they should do. Behind the giants were some very strange looking animals, which the giants seemed to be keeping as we keep dogs. There were some strange fowl, smaller than turkeys but larger than ducks, and some other beasts somewhat larger than dogs with long thick fur, some straight and some very curly, and then some great animals, larger and fatter than deer, and all the animals had the same sort of curved and pointed horns that the giants had.

There was no agreement among our people - some wanted to meet these creatures and others wanted to keep distant. Keeony said perhaps they should report this to the elders before taking any further action. Just then the giants began to come towards our people in a body, and it did not feel safe to stay, knowing so little of their intentions, and Keeony's people got into their canoes and paddled south around the headland.

No one in Keeony's village knew what to make of this story. Word of it traveled to other villages, and a number of councils took place during the winter months. People came from far places with stories we had never heard before, telling of encounters with other beings in far places we did know about. Far, far to the north, it was said, some of our hunters had met people who lived in lands of continuous snow and ice, who were covered in fur except for their little brown faces and who built ice lodges and hunted seals and walruses and ice-bears. People found these people very hospitable and generous, just like real human beings, and always liked to meet them. They in turn told of another people like themselves living on an island to the east who had fair skin and light eyes but otherwise were much like themselves. Then we heard from some daring relatives who had rowed their canoes far to the east to a place in the ocean where there were many fish, and once they had met there a very large canoe of wood with small dark men with black hair on their heads and faces, who had great nets and filled their canoe full with great fish that they then covered with salt. The sounds they made to each other were unintelligible, but with their gestures they seemed to say they had come from some place far away to the east and south.

Such tales had sometimes come up around the fires of winter storytelling, but no one knew what they meant. Some of our elders reminded us that our own people had once come from places far away. The old legends tell of our people living on islands a long time ago, where there were mountains and many fruits that grew all year, and that the people had to leave those lands when the mountains began to throw fire and ash all over themselves. They traveled a long time in many canoes and when they landed they kept together. Along the shores there were many peoples living who did not welcome them, who were threatening and hostile, so they moved ever further inland and into the mountains. For many generations our people, it was said, lived and prospered in the mountains, but then another hostile people began to come and attack their villages, killing the males and stealing the women and their stores.

Then, the stories say, the people built whole villages, like the moles and other animals, underneath their own villages, and when the enemy approached, they abandoned their houses and went underground. The enemy warriors looted what few things they could find, but there was little there, so they left and our people returned to their homes. Then after one raid the enemy decided to stay and live in the empty houses, and our people were stuck like rabbits in their warrens, able to slip out only at night. When the enemy noticed things were missing in the morning they blamed the spirits and the little people.

But our people could not live like that forever, and so one night they gathered the whole tribe and slipped out to wander again across the earth. In their wanderings they met many different people, some friendly and some hostile, and all of them said they had come from somewhere else, from the south, or from the far north across the ice, or from the sea, even from another world beneath this one. Always they sought the land that Kiehtan, the Creator, meant for them alone. Sometimes the water rose in floods and they climbed above into the mountains to where the peaks became little islands again, and when the waters receded they went down again, into the mists, crossing deserts, plains, snow and ice, moving ever north and east, and some stopped where it seemed a good place, but others kept on to find the country where Maushop lived, he who had been their first teacher. When they reached the sea many stayed and said here are the Dawn Lands promised to us, but others thought there might be better fruits further south. And so the lands became filled with many nations all speaking different dialects of the Algonquin tongue.

So we have always known that the world is much bigger than our little part of it, with oceans and islands and many different peoples living in mountains and deserts and plains and woodlands and even in the lands where the earth hides beneath ice and snow all year. But no one had ever met any people like the giants who now made their village on that estuary to the north. It was decided that a very large expedition would go in spring to see if they had stayed and survived the winter, and that we would bring many furs to see what they might trade.

And so, when the rain and storms of spring had subsided, we gathered a great fleet of canoes. Word had spread all winter, and just about every village along the coast sent a number of canoes filled with furs and curious warriors. We all gathered to spend the night just below the headland, so that we could start out and arrive together early in the morning. As Nepaushet, our Grandfather Sun, sent his first rays across the ocean our great horde of canoes rounded the headland and made for the giant's village. When they landed they held up some of the furs, showing they wanted to trade, and the giants began to bring things out of their houses.

They liked our furs very well, and we liked their spears and long knives, but they refused to trade them with us. The next wonderful thing they had was bright red material, not made from skins but woven tightly in a miraculous way so that it was smooth and soft as a good smoked buckskin. These they cut in spans as wide as our outstretched fingers, which looked fine tied about our heads, and we all traded busily, one span of red material for one fur pelt. We had very many pelts, and after a while their material began to run out, so they cut the spans to a width of only two fingers in order to get more furs. These still made excellent headbands, so trading continued briskly for a while longer.

Then all at once we heard a terrible noise, a bellowing such as a crazed moose might make, which made our blood freeze. Across from the other side of their settlement came a monster such as we had not ever encountered. It was much like the greatest of the beasts that we had seen before, but even larger, large as a moose with great humped back and with huge and fearsome head lowered, bearing those great curved horns before it, charging down the beach in our direction, snorting smoke and fire from its loathsome nostrils. One look was enough. The sight and sound of that awful monster loosed upon us had the instant effect that we left all furs we had not in our hands and ran for our lives. Before the beast had covered even a small part of the ground toward us we were back in our canoes and paddling furiously, and did not slow our pace until we were south of the headland and out of sight of that terrible creature.

It had been just past the full of Nanepaushet, Grandmother Moon, when we had set out, because of delays in bringing everyone together at the same time. We now saw that it was a mistake to begin any venture during the waning moon, as our powwauhs had warned us. Therefore we waited until the morning of the new moon before setting out again to avenge this insult. We thought the giants must have planned to drive us off in order to steal our furs when their red material had run out. This time we gathered even more warriors and canoes for our war party. We brought not only spears and bows and arrows, but also ballista, our catapults, to throw stones and leather balls and bladders. On our last visit the giants had greeted us bearing shields of white, which we took to be signs of peace, and now we believed we were right because this time they advanced upon us with shields of red. The colors of war and peace are known to all men.

There were so many of us, and our assault with arrow, spear and ballista was so ferocious that the giants were dismayed. They tried to return spear for spear, but we were like a wave rolling upon them, and they began to fall back, tripping over each other. In only a few moments they were all turned about and running away with all the speed they could bear. Naturally we began to run as well, and followed them towards their houses, which they passed without a glance and headed for the woods beyond.

As they passed a woman giant came out of one of the houses and began to shout at them. She was very angry, but not with us, with her own warriors. I think she must have been telling them to fight and calling them cowards. She was a great female, such as we have never seen, with long yellow hair in braids, but dressed also much like a warrior, with bare arms and legs and a red shield, and she carried one of those great long knives the other giants bore. It was so big it must have taken the strength of a giant to wield.

We were so amazed by the sight of this towering woman warrior that we stopped pursuing the men to look and see what she would do. She shouted at us then and waved her shield and knife in the air. We were not sure she was really a woman at first, but then we were stunned to watch her tear one of her breasts out of her garments and slap this bare breast with the great blade of her long knife while crying out a terrible war song. This appalling sight was enough for us all. Perhaps she was one of those m'teolin witches that can be either man or woman as they choose. We did not want to even imagine the magic and the medicine she was conjuring then. As one man we turned and ran for our canoes.

Keeony had picked up one of the great long-handled two-edged axes that the giants used in war, but when he tested it against a rock it broke, and so he felt it was weak and left it there. Just before dawn the next day some of the giants came upon five of our people. They had not been with us and not known about the attack or about the horrible giant witch, and they were asleep in ignorance some little ways up the river. The giants killed all of them just as they lay and stole away their pelts and their pemmican.

"And that," said Omogom, "is all of the story as it was told to me by Keeony and confirmed by the others who were with him. On a later trip in the summer our people found the giant camp abandoned, not a trace of them or their animals. We have not seen or heard of them since."

Wequash, her aunt, Suttaquin, Namset, and Omogom all stared silently into the fire for a long time. No one knew what to say. There seemed to be nothing more that might be said. But the pictures stayed in the flames and in the coals and moved and glowed there still.

The next morning Auntie thanked Suttaquin for her hospitality and Omogom for his story, and Suttaquin invited them to come again. Omogom said they should travel north and visit his village too some time. And then they were off. They talked very little on the journey that day, each in their own thoughts for which they seemed to have no words. In Shawmut their relatives asked for news of Naumkeag, but neither Wequash nor her aunt felt able to relate the giant story they had heard, so they talked only of the village and its preparations for spring.

As they drew close to their own village the following day, Wequash felt sudden little rushes of emotion every time she recognized a place, a fork in the path, a curve of the little river, a gushing spring and a freshly melted brooklet singing loudly to the woods, the cedar swamp, the fat, wide sacred birch with branches so low you could sit on them without climbing. She was glad to be coming home, but she knew that home would never feel the same secure place where everything was known. When they reached their lake they rested on a boulder, looking quietly at the peaceful waters.

"I don't think I can tell that story," Wequash said finally, "I don't want to. Maybe not ever."

"I know."

"But Mequin will ask me. And Chepacket. I had dreams last night."

"You don't have to tell them anything. Even if it were your story you would not have to tell it to anyone else unless you wanted to. Except the powwauh."

"Should I tell the powwauh?"

"Only if you want to. Because it's not your story. If it were your story you would need to understand it, and you would need to tell it."

"But I want to understand it."

"Come then."

But at the powwauh's wetu it was Auntie who told the story. Wequash only could nod to confirm the strange parts of it. At the end of the story the elderly powwauh sat very still for so long that Wequash thought he might have fallen asleep, and wondered if he had heard at all.

"It is indeed a strange story," the old man said at last. "But it is not our story. I do not think we have anything to do with this story. I will not forget it, however. Perhaps we will hear other stories in the future that will bring this to light. For now I think it is enough for our people that we continue to walk the path that Kiehtan has given us, that Maushop showed to us, and that Weetucks reminded us about. Perhaps this has something to do with the prophecies left us by Weetucks. We must wait and see."

As they left the old man's wetu, Wequash walked slowly, in silence. She should have told the powwauh her dream. But perhaps he would think her foolish. Who was she to have a dream of any importance? She couldn't even tell Auntie about the dream. Her aunt waited and watched her for a while before she asked what her niece was thinking.

"I don't know what to think. Suddenly the whole world seems different and strange."

49

"To me too."

"That's what I mean. Before when I didn't know or understand something I knew it was because I was still young. But I knew I could ask you and you would explain. Or if the truth was beyond your knowledge we could ask a sagamore or a powwauh. But here is a mystery that not even the powwauh understands."

"Just now I think it would be good to be alone for a while. I'm going to walk back to the lake."

Wequash nodded. She understood. Now that she thought about it, she wanted to think by herself too. She walked back to her family's wetu alone. Her father and her uncles were in the woods somewhere hunting, and her brothers were playing somewhere with their friends. Granny was also off somewhere. Her mother and her other aunts were preparing food on the other end, and the old people were napping. Wequash sat on her bed.

Everything was familiar. The smells, the sounds, the feel of the elk robe beneath her. But something had changed. What was it? It was as though now suddenly everything seemed - not unreal, but - impermanent? Yes. Fragile. Ephemeral. As if the whole scene before her, the three fires, the wetu, the whole village were built out of smoke and might just fade like haze before her eyes. She had never felt like this before, and she didn't know what to do with the feeling.

She was so distracted she didn't even notice when the moose-robe door opened and someone had come in. Suddenly someone was sitting beside her on the bed, and she was surprised to look up and see that it was Granny, smiling at her.

"Your thoughts look very deep, my granddaughter. Can you share them?"

"It's hard, Granny. I have feelings but I do not understand them."

"Do you know where they come from, these feelings?"

"From the story of the giants. The one I asked you about. Auntie and I heard about them in Naumkeag."

"I have heard. From your aunt, and from the powwauh. It is a strange story indeed. Come and tell me about it as I make succotash."

"I have so many questions now that no one can answer," Wequash followed Granny back to her own fire, talking all the while. "Where do they come from? How do they live? Why do they come? Are there others like them? I want to know, but also I don't. Because I want them to stay away."

Granny said nothing but began scooping dried corn into a ceramic pot.

"It's much worse than the stories of the giants who became mountains and those old stories, because this happened now, to people we are related to."

"You feel frightened."

"It's not like any fear I have felt before. There is something, and no one has heard of it before. Now it has come close to us. There is something very dangerous. It's not something we know. Not something we can prepare for. Our world has no

50

such beings, but it seems there is a world beyond this one. This world may be full of giants and monsters. Now they have found us they can come again."

Granny nodded and began to pour water from a buckskin water-bag into the clay pot.

"I dreamed last night, Granny. I dreamed that Weetucks was warning us again. I dreamed that there were villages in flames, children crying in the smoke, and blood spilled on the earth. I dreamed the giants were tearing down all the trees, poisoning the water, killing the animals, and we had to live in their square boxes and we were prisoners in our own land."

Wequash was shivering now. Granny put an arm around her.

"Come, Granddaughter, help me here. Get out that pot of soaked beans over there and pour them in with the corn, then take the stick and pile coals around the bottom of the pot."

Wequash could not speak while she concentrated on doing the task well and not spilling the beans. In that concentration her mind also quieted, and she sighed.

"Sit with me a while, Granddaughter." Granny patted the ground beside her. When she sat and felt her grandmother's arm pull her close Wequash leaned over and put her head in the older woman's lap. Something about this closeness, the warmth and tenderness that she had known since childhood, and Wequash suddenly felt a rush of tears to her eyes. Granny patted her shoulder to comfort her and she began to sob, hugging her grandmother's legs tightly.

"Am I foolish, Granny? What should I do? What shall we all do?" she managed in a few moments.

"Weeping is good sometimes. It clears the head. Then we will cook the succotash. What we must do is survive. Plant the three sisters, care for them, harvest them, cook them, and survive. As Kiehtan the Creator has taught us. Follow Kiehtan's instructions, learn all we can of this world and live in it in a good way."

With another great sob Wequash sat up and put her arms around her grandmother and squeezed with all her strength.

"Oh, Granny, I love you so much. I love our village, our family, everyone, the woods, the lake, I want it like this forever."

"I know, granddaughter."

"Thank you, Granny. I feel better now."

Wequash let out a deep breath. She stood and put her hands on her hips.

"Time to stir the succotash," she said.

APPONAUG

for Burne and the girls

This really happened.

In the sea of time the tides only run in one direction. They recede from the tide-pools of memory to flood unsuspecting shores beyond. Here are the wiggles caught in one small pool.

Two girls are poking driftwood sticks, bleached and smooth, into a shallow remnant of warm sea-water. They are in early adolescence, already stretching towards the full height of their tall and long-legged people. For clothing they wear only pieces of smoke-softened deerskin tied at the waist. One only, the larger of the two, has small new prominences of growing breasts. Their lean bare bodies are the color of cedar wood, and their black hair hangs loosely below their shoulders.

These girls are alone on the ebb-tide flats, half-way between the white dunes and the bay, murmuring far beyond. Sandpipers strut across the wet sand, and terns skim and dart just above them. The sun has yet to appear over the great dunes to the east. For all the People of the First Light it is the time of the nikkomo, or feast, of the Sequanakeeswash, the Spring Moon, which is their New Year's ceremony.

The girls are probing for some mysterious life-form that has dug itself down from the bottom of the pool, but it eludes them. They investigate several other such pools with quiet curiosity. The larger girl, Maskeegsy, by name, suddenly looks out towards the distant bay and speaks.

"The tide will turn soon We must dig our quahogs now, because the sea returns fast over these flats."

They begin to tramp around on the sand, and wherever little jets of water spurt up they stop and dig swiftly until they retrieve a prize of a hard-shelled clam.

There are canoes in the bay, a number of women wading and groping around in the shoals, and other children along the beach digging clams. People from many small villages further down the cape have been up and moving for hours, stalking the woods for game, unloading the fish weirs. All are moving towards this narrow arm of the cape, where from the top of the highest hills you can see the ocean to the east and the bay to the west. On a meadow protected by woods and dunes, fire pits are being dug and the last of the winter food stores being brought out for the great feast.

As the girls harvest more and more quahogs from the sand they become more talkative.

"Is your sister there with the lobstering women now?" Maskeegsy asks?

"No." Aquaya, the smaller one, answers, "She strips the dried corn and cooks it with the last of the year's dried beans for succotash Autaquay learns more of the Sequanakeeswash Nikkomo with the grandmothers and the aunts." Aquaya sighs, repeating an aunt's admonition, "She has a lot to learn."

"Hasn't she done it before?"

"We help every year with the preparations, but she never paid attention. Always dreaming, thinking of other things."

"Boys." Maskeegsy agreed.

"I know more about the first feast of the new year than she, and she is three years older."

"Now Autaquay must learn how to care for a home, feed a family."

"I remember her always mooning about some boy, from Nobscusset, wasn't he?"

"Funny that now she marries someone she doesn't know at all. And not even from the cape - from somewhere in Pokonoket country. How did they ever meet anyway?"

"Oh, she saw him at the Nikkomo last fall. You know, the big one, Sachmiawene, the harvest feast and council called by the Great Sachem of the Pokonoket. This young Assonet kept smiling at our family. Really trying to watch Autaquay without being noticed. He even spoke to her, but I think she did not answer."

"Didn't she like him?"

"Maybe not at first. Or I think she was really afraid. I don't understand why girls get so afraid to speak to boys, but she who cannot stop chattering could say nothing to this stranger."

"Yet she will marry him."

"Who could understand my sister? When this boy sent word to our father that he would like to marry Autaquay, she agreed. She did not have to. Our father would never force us to marry anyone. He did say that the boy's family was well-known, his father an important panesis, and that his clan uncles spoke well of the boy."

"Did you see him at the Nikkomo?"

"I suppose so, but I wouldn't remember. I can't look at any of those boys for long. They are so stupid. Pretending to be braver, stronger, finer than anyone, looking down on all the girls."

"Well, you'll marry one some day."

"Not one of those strutting pheasants! I'll wait till they grow up and see if any of them gets bearable. Or maybe I'll just never get married."

"Aquaya!"

"I don't know what happens to girls. One day they are perfectly sensible, and then some boy looks at them, and they stop thinking and talking and making sense. Well, Autaquay never made much sense to me, but at least she could talk."

56

"How does it feel to be going to have a brother you haven't met living here?"

"I don't know. He just better not be one of those who wants his wife's sister to be another wife for him."

"I don't believe you hate boys so much really. What about Chogan?"

"Your brother's different." Aquaya glances towards the bay, as if to be sure Chogan is not able to see them - to sense they are talking about him. His canoe is not yet in sight. "He's like family, like a cousin. We all grew up together, and he's - well, he's not like those others."

"See?"

"Doesn't mean I want to marry him. Why are we talking about marriage, anyway?"

"Maybe you're still too young to think about those things. You'll feel different when you come into your first moon-time."

"How do you know? You haven't yourself yet."

"Well, it's very soon, I'm sure, I thought it might come now at the full moon. There is no spot of blood anywhere, but I can feel a strange new power, and I know it will be soon that I must go stay in the Moon Lodge and receive woman instructions from Clan Mother and my aunties. See, I am already filling out on top, and you still look like a boy there."

"Do you really feel power in you now?"

"Oh, yes. Well, not all the time. But sometimes, I am sure of it. Especially today - Grandmother Moon will bring me the purification to prepare my body to make babies. That's why it is such a sacred time, when the full power of Kiehtan, the Creator, moves in us women. Grandma says that's why the powwauh won't let us near the ceremonies when we are on our moon. Our power is too great, and we unbalance him."

"I can believe that. Women are already more powerful than men anyway."

"Oh, Aquaya, you are really funny! I mean, why is it that men are the warriors, to protect us? You don't see women going out to hunt the great whales - or tracking the great bears. You just say things to be outrageous and make people laugh."

"Well, I know I'm stronger than any of the boys my age. I can run faster, and I can throw them on the ground even if I am smaller. Even Chogan."

"Aha - you'd like that, wouldn't you?"

Again Aquaya is compelled to glance out to the canoes clustered around the fish weirs in the bay.

"Well," she says, "I suppose you think I haven't noticed you watching that new young visitor, that Maquas boy."

"What do you know about him?"

"Not much. I guess we'll find out from your brother. See - that's him there - in Chogan's mishoon."

* * * *

The mishoon, or dugout canoe, she points at is just now putting out of the little estuary, heading for the weirs, which look like masses of little sticks sprouting from the waters of the bay a mile off-shore. In this canoe are two boys, Maskeegsy's older brother, Chogan, and the visitor, a Mohawk, or Maquas, in their Nauset language, both asserting themselves grimly to digging their paddles quickly in the bay and pulling water hard behind them. They are both conscious of being the last ones out, and they know they will have to take a lot of teasing from the older boys and young men who have been out there some time clearing the weirs.

The speed of the dugout gliding over the wavelets and the soft gurgling song it sings attracts a small pod of porpoises, who hurry happily to the chase, and race alongside, bobbing in and out of the water, sprouting fine sprays of water that sound like little sneezes, running ahead to ride the currents pushed forward by the canoe, then, impatient with their slowness, dive to make a game of circling the canoe, or thumping playfully against its underside.

Chogan, the smaller of the two boys, who paddles from the guiding position behind, laughs and calls out to the porpoises, "Ho! Tatackomauog! There you are! You are late - even lazier than we this morning. But we cannot stop now to play. If we get some small fish we will save them for you."

The larger boy in the forward position is startled to see a porpoise leap from the water beside him and seem to look him straight in the eye.

"What is that?" he cries out.

"Huh," says the first, "that is a Tatackom. I forget that you Maquas have no ocean near you and do not know our sea people. The tatackomauog are special friends of mine and my spirit guides as well. They are playful and curious, but they are also shy creatures and do not come to everyone, yet they know my canoe and come to me whenever I go out. My clan uncle presented them to me when I was a baby and asked them to watch over me." The Mohawk nods, showing he understands. They paddle on in earnest silence.

As they come to the weirs, they receive the barrage of joking and teasing they expect for being late. Most vocal are the boys only a little older than they, who question what they have been up to the night before, their abilities in seamanship, how difficult it must have been for them to locate the bay, the remarkable sleeping habits of Mohawks, and various references to their age, strength and alertness. The comments of the middle-aged are more spare and more dry, but still good humored. The older men do not comment but chuckle merrily at all the jokes.

The boys find a vacant spot in the circle of canoes about the weirs and tie up. The Mohawk boy now sees that the weirs, which looked from shore like a bunch of little sticks, are really long poles made from stripped trunks of pine from the inner woods where they grow tall. These had been driven close together into the sand far below the waves, in rows that create a maze of channels so that fish could swim in but they were not clever enough to find their way out again. In the center the fish are so thick you can spear them, or sweep them in a net, or even reach in and pull big ones out by the tail. The boys join the others in spearing out fish and in a little while their canoe is filled. Now Chogan takes a net he has made of sinew on instruction of his clan uncle, and sweeps it through the inner waters of the weir, pulling out many smaller fish.

As they pull away from the weir, Chogan turns the mishoon towards the outer bay and begins to whistle. The Mohawk looks at him with an expression that says, "What now?"

"Be patient, Maquas, and keep watching the sea."

Maquas, of course, is not how he would be known to his people, who call themselves Ganienkehaga, the People of the Flint, but he has been among the Dawnland People so long that he has accepted Maquas as his name among them.

The fish are stirring and flopping in the bottom of the dugout. Maquas wonders aloud if they should not be getting the fish to shore while they are still alive and fresh. Chogan just splashes a little sea water over the fish and goes on whistling. Maquas looks at the distant beach and the broad reach of the bay ahead. Even though the water is smooth with only occasional darker patches of breeze ruffling it here and there, the Mohawk looks uneasy. He has never been so far from land on such a wide expanse of water before.

Suddenly he notices something ahead and off to their right, about a hundred paces away, if one could walk the sea. Is it something floating there? Some flotsam, a bit of a tree? - Now it's gone - no, there it is again, moving slowly, and it is shiny-black. Now Maquas can see it is the curved hook of a fin - and there is another now at its side, and another and another! Now there are six fins, close to each other, and all moving slowly towards the land. Or perhaps towards the fish weirs.

"Look there - there they are!" Maquas points.

"No," Chogan keeps looking all around the canoe. "That is not Tatackom. That is his uncle Pootop the whale."

"How can you tell? From here they look the same."

"Tatackom doesn't lie still like that. The tatackomauog move and move, very fast. And they have only a small point of a fin low on the back. This pootopoag, these black ones here in the bay, they have a big hooked fin, as you see, and are much, much slower. They are much bigger - big as two of our bigger canoes. Like Tatackom, Pootop travels in little bands or clans, and is both curious and friendly. These Pootapoag are more shy, but I have swum with them too."

"Do you hunt them?"

"No. We hunt the great whales that live in the ocean beyond. They are even bigger, twice as big. These bay creatures are like neighbors, like family. They come to our canoes and travel with us for company. They swim right in on full tides and stay on the beach as the tide goes out. Then we must get to them quickly. If we cannot get them back out to sea they will die. Then we have to cut the meat and cook it. Because a rotting carcass of one of these big fellows will smell so you won't want to come near the beach for a long time. You have never smelled anything so strong and so terrible!

As Chogan speaks the whales turn and begin to move toward the canoe, as if responding to his speech. The fins sometimes come higher and then part of an arching back is seen rolling up and then disappearing under the water completely, reappearing a minute later further along. They move in rhythm with each other, two or three appearing and disappearing here and there together. As they get closer they snort little sprays of water as they exhale through the blow holes on their backs. Then suddenly they are gone.

"Look!" Chogan says. Maquas looks straight down where Chogan points and is astounded to see a whole silent herd of whales passing smoothly just below the canoe. They are twenty to thirty feet long, but there are also several babies only a few feet long moving close by their mothers' sides.

"They could upset us easily!" Maquas cries.

"Yes. But they never do. They trust us - we never harm them. It would be bad luck. They scare fish our way, and we give them squid. And sometimes we help them out of the shallows so they won't get beached."

Now the whales have appeared again, far beyond the canoe, heading down the bay. Suddenly something thumps the bottom of the dugout, and it rolls sharply.

"Ah, there you are! I told you we'd be back." Chogan begins throwing the very small fish into the water, and the porpoise pod dives and splashes and snorts and slaps their tails as the wriggling fish dart about.

"I can never figure out if they eat these fish or just play with them. Anyway they like it. Well, we've paid our respects - now let's get back."

* * * *

A line of twenty or so women are wading waist-deep along a sandbar some ways off shore. Every few moments one of them will stoop over, reaching arm, shoulder and head down into the water and emerge with a wriggling lobster in her hand which she places in the basket strapped to her side. These crustaceans are so plentiful in these shallows at low tide that in a very short while their baskets have become nearly full. They have begun a song of thanks to the shellfish world which is borne across the waters to the men in their canoes at the weirs and to the women turning the soil on the hillside gardens above. The sky is clear and gentle, the breeze soft and playful, the sun high and proud, a distant chief guarding the life of his people.

On the beach Aquaya and Maskeegsy have their large bags they had fashioned from fish-nets so full they are too heavy to carry and they must be dragged across the sand. When they reach the inlet they wade inland waist-deep through the water, allowing the buoyancy of the salt water to lighten their burdens. Tying the bags of quahogs in the water to stakes that would be seen above the high tide, the girls ascend to a prominence above the inlet where a number of people have already gathered. They seek out their mothers who are bearing branches hung with dried corn and baskets full of dried beans to where a long trench now contains a smoking fire from one end to the other. The girls march beside their mothers, listening to their giggling gossip.

Over near the fire pits Autaquay, the bride, seems deep in thought as she scrapes the dried kernels from the corn cobs she takes off a pile beside her. The other women look over at her now and then from their activities, but do not interrupt the long thoughts they see must be playing out in the bride's mind. Last night the elder women of her clan have talked with her about the responsibilities of marriage, what to expect of a husband, what to accept and what to insist upon, and in all giving more answers than she had questions for. Today she has much to think over, and preparing food is a good time for thought.

She cuts the kernels from the cobs vigorously, as though they were withholding from her some knowledge which she would tear from them. As if Sister Corn should hold the essential secret of life. The elder women - her aunts, her grandmother, and her clan mother - they speak as the voice of propriety, of what is proper and what is expected. But when night comes no elders and no relatives will be with her, only this young man whom she does not really know.

What will he expect, what will he know, will he be patient and understanding? Now she can hardly remember anything that he said when he spoke to her during the Rabbit Dance. It was women's choice, and she had rashly chosen him because she had seen him looking at her. Truth, Autaquay, you know you peeked over at him before as well. He really was beautiful. He had to dance with her, or pay a penalty, but he had seemed happy to have been chosen, and he chattered away all through the dance so that she, who had used all her boldness in the choosing, did not have to say one word.

She knew then somehow that when she slipped away later to walk alone by the river he would follow. As she sat watching the current the drum in her heart beat wildly, feeling his presence near. But over her heart she heard the song of the flute, his flute. Just behind her playing softly, only for her. It was the way of courting, and suddenly this man, the dance, the walk, the flute - it all rushed upon her so quickly. There were so many feelings, feelings never felt, and a great mystery that now entered her life.

That mystery had engulfed her, and she stands within it now. Preparing a feast for her wedding. She knew that he would ask her parents, through her father, and that this stranger, this Assonet, already knew she would consent. He knew that when her father asked her she would say yes. It was designed so in the patterns of Creation. A mystery.

She sighs and picks up the stone knife and begins again scraping the kernels into a ceramic bowl of brown beans, then to be cooked for succotash, with only a little taste of fat from woodchuck or porcupine. A strange thought startle her - soon she will be doing this for her husband, perhaps making a stew of it with squash and pumpkin and game or fish that he has caught. And then for a child - for children - that will grow and help until some day they too will marry and do this, and think these thoughts, and be filled with confusion and curiosity and terror as she is now....and then have their own children and she, Autaquay, will be a grandmother and an elder like Clan Mother.

She looks at the morning sun, still vague and pale behind the sea's mist rising over the dunes.

"Grandfather," she prays, "move very slowly and give me time to get used to these things."

* * * *

The light of morning, already so advanced on the bay and the shore where the feast is being prepared, is only just beginning to penetrate the deep tangled thicket of a forest not far from there. There a young man has been sitting very still in a hollow since he left the first false light of dawn on the beach and crawled in the dark into this thicket. In his hand is his bow, string fitted, arrow nocked. He stares through the woven branches of the low scrub oak at a larger tree whose outlines are beginning to become clear in the advancing light. Slowly, slowly, without a sound, he is drawing back the arrow which is aimed toward that tree. It is fully drawn now just as a dark shape on a low branch standing out from the trunk stirs just slightly. And now there is the loud snap of the bowstring and the whisper of the arrow as it brushes the leaves and disappears into the black shape towards which it was directed. The shape briefly unfolds great dark wings, but they are useless as the body to which they are attached topples heavily to the ground.

The young man is Attuck, deer clan, son of Espaquin, panesis of Assonet. He strides quickly forward, retrieves his arrow with a wrench, picks up his turkey by the legs, wings flapping lifelessly, and strides back to the mishoon he left pulled up on the beach beyond the dunes.

Dropping his prize beside the other gifts in the canoe, fur pelts of weasel, beaver and fisher, and strings of purple wampum beads, he pushes it into the stream emptying through the tidal flats, drags it along that purring little current through the long wet sands of the low tide flats to the deeper water of the bay. There is no breeze yet as he sets off towards his destination further down the cape where it bends at a right angle to the north and larger dunes begin to rise.

The sun has risen above the land ahead, but is still obscured by morning fog. He tries to fill his mind only with the deep long strokes of his paddling, the swarming of gulls arguing above in the pale blue summer sky emerging from the thinning fog, the shining calm of the early morning waters, and the dark indications of the weirs standing out far ahead which will guide him to his destination.

To concentrate on his task only he begins to sing a canoe song, steadying the long sweeps of his paddle to the rhythm of the song. Yet he is unable to block from his thoughts the image of the young woman whom has known for such a little time, only some moments at different times during the Nikkomo ceremonies, during the Rabbit Dance and at a few meals and one chance meeting by the river. A meeting that as it proved changed his life forever. After those few talks, and some nights of thinking about her, he was rash enough to ask her to marry (through her parents, as was proper). This young woman whose face he can hardly recall, but whose words and whose laughter echo in his mind, who waits ahead for him now, waiting for a ceremony that will change both their lives.

His most of all, since he will leave his village and his family to make a home with her in this strange place and become part of her family and her village. He knows her people, most of them, from seeing them at ceremonies and dances in different places in summer. Feeling the desire to begin his true life and fulfillment with a family of his own making, and finding none of the young Assonet women suitable, he had begun to travel to as many dances and ceremonies in other places as he could, to observe the marriageable daughters of other villages.

When he saw Autaquay he looked no further. She was tall, strong of build rather than delicate, but with a grace to her movements that put him in mind of the melodies he practiced on his cedar flute. He had made the flute just with the idea of courting, and as he mused upon it by himself in the bush and by the shores of the Titicut River, letting his breath and his fingers and the flute follow the warm, mellow tones, he became one with the long wistful tunes he spun. All his longing and desire was beginning to come together in the songs of his flute. Seeing Autaquay, struck by the life in her eyes and in her movements and by the fact that she had chosen him for the Rabbit Dance, although during the dance she would not speak and only responded to his prattle with a shy smile, he had known at last for whom his melodies were intended. And for the first time he allowed another human being to hear and know his heart crying through his flute.

Now when he looks at the unfamiliar shoreline ahead getting closer, the cluster of canoes around the weirs becoming visible, seeing that the tiny specks on the beach are slowly moving and must be people, now catching sight of other specks wading in the water off shore, and smoke rising behind the dunes, what had seemed unreal becoming real, the immensity of the occasion begins to rise in him like an unnamed fear. This is a day unlike any he has known in his life. He has no experience, no preparation to hold on to. Grimly he digs his paddle deeper with each stroke, applying trust in physical effort to steady his thoughts and his resolve. If he takes care to do what he must do the event will take care of itself, will carry him forward, like the mishoon.

He realizes these thoughts have driven his paddling, digging his paddle in the water harder and faster with every stroke, and he is racing. If he keeps that up he will be exhausted when he gets there. He stops. Takes a long breath. Looks again at the shore, the black specks taking human shape now, the canoes heading for the inlet, the smoke from several fires now standing up from behind the dunes. He starts to sing again, and to resume paddling at a slow even rate.

He smiles to himself. Now he understands why his father and uncles tried to persuade him to travel with his family to the Nauset Sequanakeeswash Nikkomo. They knew the feelings he would be having at this time and wanted him to be with his own people until the ceremonies. But he had wanted to make this trip alone, to bring his gifts, his weapons, his flute and personal things in his own mishoon, and he wanted to face his feelings and confusions by himself. He is glad he is alone now, taking this time to feel it all. He is the only one who will live this life. No one else can learn it for him, or can understand it. To be a man, to be himself, he must learn and master it for himself.

He had paddled from the Pokonoket shores on the previous day, camping on the beach and rising before dawn to creep quietly into the scrub oak growth to hunt, after singing his wish to Kiehtan that some animal relative might come forth to give himself to the wedding feast. It augured well for this marriage that he was guided directly to the turkey waiting quietly for him in the dark branches of the night-tree. He had already been at sea when this day was rising anew out of the fog. The calm of that day, of the pale sky and still waters of the bay, pacified the turmoil of his thoughts but seemed to him another world, one he was only passing through to a new life. On the land rising slowly ahead was the reality of his future. He really was going to live there, in that unknown place, among those unknown people, share a wetu with an unknown young woman he had barely met, leave behind his Assonet identity and become a Nauset. Was that ever possible? It seems so strange. But it is the way of their people, Dawnland people, people of the east, who first see the sun arise from the sea.

After all, he is a responsible man, son of a panesis. An Assonet , one of the respected Pokonoket villages, of the People of the First Light, the Wampanoag, as are the Nauset. This place, the bay, the long flat beaches, the dunes, the wide sky, they are different from the place of his woodland village by the little stream that leads to the Titicut, but these people are one with his own, with the same language and customs, the same stories and legends. It will not be so very great a change to live in their village.

Yes, that is the important thing. He is a responsible man. He will be hunter and fisher and warrior and son-in-law and husband and father and grandfather one day among these people. Whatever comes he will learn and he will master. He will be responsible.

It is a good thought, and his song rings clear over the waters.

* * * *

It is now many hours later. The sun has nearly reached its zenith. An offshore breeze has picked up, gaining strength as it crossed the bay, freshening what would otherwise have been a hot day. The people, Nausets and guests, visitors from Pokonoket and Capawak, are gathering at the meeting place, making a large circle around the sacred fire. Only a few women have stayed behind, to watch over the many clay pots of succotash bubbling on the long fire within a slit trench.

The powwauh, a dark, thin old man who earlier had seemed weary, bent and slow, now stands tall in his regalia of animal furs, wolf bonnet with four dangling turkey feathers, copper armbands, wampum belt across a shoulder, wampum necklaces, various pouches for tobacco, sweet grass, cedar and other herbs and a medicine bag hanging at his breast. Years seem to have fallen from him as now he strides around the fire, stopping to throw a bit of tobacco in it at the four directions, with a mumbled prayer to each. Now he stops and looks around. The people are settling into place around the circle. The elders are all seated. The Nauset sachem nods to signal all are ready.

The powwauh raises his hands and looks up to the sky, calling out in a loud clear voice greetings to the sun and all the unknown beings beyond his domain, to Mother Earth and all her children, the human beings and their relatives, the plant and animal people. He says they are all grateful for this good day, for their lives and the good health of their families, for the good year that has just passed, and for the continuing harmony of the web of life as they enter into a new year in contentment and joy. He asks that Kiehtan, that spirit containing all spirits, that sang the universe into being, that sets the rhythms and the melodies for all the dance of Creation, accept the grateful thanksgivings of his little grandchildren gathered here in circle to mark the passing of another year and give birth to yet another cycle of the seasons of planting, growing, harvesting, and dreaming.

The people murmur a vocable of assent that sounds like "huh!" or perhaps "ho! " or "ha!' or even "hau!" or "a-ho!" There are some moments of quiet as the listeners wait, absorbing what has been said, looking into the ground or up into the sky, feeling what this day contains.

The Nauset sachem now steps forward to greet again the visitors from other villages and thanks everyone for coming to honor the growing powers of Mother Earth, and acknowledge Grandfather Sun that warms her, Grandmother Moon still growing, by whose cycles they must plant, the great Bird of Thunder with his children. Cloud, Wind, and Rain , and to bless the soon to be planted seeds of the Three Sisters, Corn, Beans, and Squash.

These ceremonies, together with a final farewell to those of their nation whose spirits departed to walk the star path during the past year, a welcome to those new spirits who have come into the families of the nation in the past year, and the giving of names to those in need of them, will all take place tomorrow. Today there will be, before the sun reaches its highest point, during the period of its greatest power, a ceremony to welcome a new relative into the village and join him in marriage to one of their daughters. Afterwards the nikkomo, which has been being prepared and cooked all morning, will begin and he hopes there will be more than enough to make all the honored guests joyful and glad they came.

Now the sachem turns towards the women's side, points to Aquaya and she runs to him.

"What is it, uncle?'

"It is time. Run to the Moon Lodge and tell your clan mother we are ready for the ceremony now."

Aquaya is off, scampering eagerly out of the ceremonial area and over the hill. In the women's lodge Autaquay is having her hair twined with strings of shell beads and partridge feathers by one of the aunts, while her clan mother, old Misesquaw, is painting the bride's face with a design of yellow, ochre, and turquoise. Her brush is a twig that has been crushed by a stone on one end, and her colors are made from ground flowers mixed with water and a little clay.

"They are ready!" Aquaya announces, unable to completely conceal the excitement in her voice.

"Good. And so are we," Misesquaw pronounces, stepping back to appraise her handiwork. "Now we go. Stay by my side, Autaquay. I will be slow, to show we are not too eager, but relaxed, to show that we are comfortable and all is well."

Now Autaquay steps from the Moon Lodge together with her clan mother, followed by her sister Aquaya and the aunties who were helping the bride prepare. Autaquay wears a soft doeskin skirt that has been blanched and dyed very light, almost white. Above her waist she wears many strings of beads of wampum, seed husk, and ceramic, a choker of bone and shell, and copper armbands. As they near the ceremonial ground other members of her family join the procession, uncles, cousins, grandparents, and at the end, her mother and father. Her father carries a large basket filled with many things wrapped in skins which he places beside him as the family stands together in the center.

Now from the other side of the arbor comes Attuck with those of his family that have made the journey from their Pokonoket village, his father, Espaquin, panesis of Assonet, his mother, Wunnuta, his three brothers, his grandfathers, two of his uncles, and a few older cousins. The trip had been too long for all the small children in the family, so his aunts and grandmothers had stayed behind to care for them.

The two families stand facing each other east and west of the center, with the powwauh between them. Attuck has also painted his face in a lively and festive way. He wears a buckskin loincloth and a fox skin draped over one shoulder, beaded necklaces, bone and shell choker, copper armbands, and a headdress that features two-pronged horns of a very young deer.

"These two families have come here today," the powwauh announces to the onlookers, "to join two of their children. These families will thus be united, and at the same time another family will be created. Though their villages are at some distance, they are all of our people, the Wampanoag, the People of the Morning Light, and the children of this new family will bring honor and strength to all of us."

Aquaya looks at her sister. Autaquay looks more beautiful than she could have imagined. It is more than the painted face, the extra beads and feathers. There seems to be a soft light that glows around her, or within her, like a reflection of sunlight. Autaquay does not look at the powwauh, but straight ahead of her. Aquaya wonders if her sister is afraid. If she is it doesn't show.

Aquaya glances at Attuck. He is looking at Autaquay with a serious expression. Not really at her, because that would be rude. But you can tell as he looks from the powwauh to her father and uncles and the others of her family that he lingers a bit longer as his gaze reaches Autaquay. Aquaya sees her sister glance over at Attuck and catches him looking at her. He smiles, and Autaquay looks down to the ground. Then Attuck sees Aquaya looking at them and smiles.

Aquaya knows she should look away, but for some reason she does not but calmly stares back. He smiles more broadly at her and looks back to the powwauh, who is concluding his speech to the assembled guests. Maybe, thinks Aquaya, Attuck will not be such a bad brother-in-law after all.

Now the powwauh brings the groom and the bride out from their family groups and places them side by side. Around their shoulders he drapes a large elk-skin robe, telling them that the elk is strong but gentle, and that the bull will always protect his family and his people. Then he places a hood made from a white wolf, with tail and head, the powwauh's prize pelt, Aquaya knew, used only for very special ceremonies.

"Wolf over your heads, as he is over us all. Wolf is the spirit of the People of the First Light, our most ancient teacher. Family is the teaching of the wolf people. Family, the beginning of clan and tribe.

"In the wolf family male and female are equal. To be a parent is the highest good and the greatest responsibility. Mother and father work side by side, as equals, each one hunting and protecting and nurturing the little ones equally. If either one should die, the other becomes both mother and father and carries on. There is still much we can learn from these relatives. Their loyalty and devotion and sense of honor are beyond other animals. And, of course, like us, they may often have women sachems to lead their tribes."

The powwauh takes from his basket a stick the size of a pestle covered with the white fur of a snowshoe hare, and asks the couple to grasp it together with the hand closest to each other. Then with a thong of buckskin dyed red he wraps their wrists together.

"Now you are bound," he says, "in the sight of all your people. Red is the tie of your hearts and the blood of your new family that runs together. The fur of the hare you hold confers the blessing of many and healthy children. Now you each may speak, if you wish."

Now the couple look in each other's eyes for the first time in public, then Autaquay giggles and hides her face in his shoulder. Attuck looks around the circle as if for escape, but there is none. He must speak, but it is the moment he has been dreading.

"Honored powwauh," he nods toward the ceremonial leader, "great sachem and people of Nauset, my new relatives, please forgive my speech. I am unused to speaking before so many, so I will not try your patience long with my stuttering. Eagerly I paddled my Mishoon all the way from the Titicut to give myself and what little I have to your daughter Autaquay. And all through the journey I asked myself, what have I to give to be so blessed? My skills as hunter and fisher are modest and as warrior I am untried. All I have truly is my vow to provide for and protect my new family with all my abilities, humble though they may be. And for

68

my new father and my other new relatives, I can offer only my willing service and these few small trinkets in these baskets."

He now nods to his father who carries the two large baskets that sit beside him over and places them in front of Aquaya's father, who smiles broadly and embraces the panesis and his son. Clearly he is pleased with the speech of his new son-in-law and looks proudly around. Then Autaquay shyly murmurs a few words that have been taught to her and she has rehearsed to her clan mother, but which no one at all beyond Attuck can hear. He seems well pleased with her words though and strokes his bride's hair as she again buries her face in his chest.

The powwauh now makes a little speech to the two families, telling them to welcome this new family among them, that it joins them all into one family. He tells the circle that they are all family, and that if these young people ever find themselves in hard times, loosing house, canoe, garden, or having other troubles, that all should be ready to take them in and help them as one of their own. He wishes them good children, healthy babies, which he says also will be children of all the people, and cared for by each as their own.

Then Autaquay's father makes a little speech of his own, welcoming not only Attuck but all his Assonet family. He signals and, since he has no sons, two of his brothers bring up the baskets he has kept by him, and he offers each item in them, tools, weapons, furs, beaded belts, necklaces, chokers, copper bracelets, robes, first to the Assonet guests, then to each person in the circle. The give-away concluded, the powwauh speaks a final prayer and says it is time for the nikkommo.

* * * *

A short time later everyone is eating. The people are spread out in little groups near the cooking area. It is past noon, but the spring sunlight is not so warm that anyone seeks shade, but is rather glad for what feels like a very loving and gentle caress of its soft rays. There is a hum of voices and laughter as each little group is exchanging bits of news, exaggerated stories of the preparation for the feast, humorous comments on the wedding ceremony and the bearing of bride and groom, and jokes about the give-aways, and the expectations and realities of married life.

Aquaya lingers in passing each group, trying to learn from their joking a little more understanding of the mysteries of the nuptial event and what is expected of a young girl when she becomes a wife. She doesn't think she will get much information from Autaquay. Her sister has never been one to confide her inner feelings to anyone. Well, perhaps to her own friends, but certainly never to her little sister. Now that she is a wife, she has entered another world, Aquaya can feel it. She seems even more separated from Autaquay now as she watches her sister sitting with her new husband in the center of a group of joking friends. Autaquay seems a different person from the one who used to act so silly and to tease her and criticize her and tell her what to do. Now she is sitting so calm and self-assured, smiling indulgently while listening quietly to the others joking. As though she were already a matron; as though she already knows some secret that Aquaya can not even guess at. Mysterious. And annoying.

Aquaya hurries back to the great pots sitting in the ashes and dips two more bowls of succotash and stew to take back to the elders. That is one good new thing, anyway. This is the first time she has been asked to serve the elders, an honor reserved for older young people who can carry food quickly and neatly and will remember to come back and ask if they want anything more and clean up after them. She and Maskeegsy and several other girls about their age are scurrying back and forth from the fires to where the old people are sitting under a shady arbor.

On the way to get her own stew now, Aquaya glances again at her sister and is amazed to see her laughing and putting bits of lobster in Attuck's mouth while he is doing the same to her. They are awkward because they are both laughing so much, and Aquaya shakes her head and turns away, almost colliding with Maskeegsy.

"Come on," her friend urges, "the old ones have enough for now."

"Yes, I'm going to get my own bowl now," Aquaya returns.

"I already filled both our bowls and put them over there." She points, and Aquaya looks, a little mystified, to where her own bowl steams with succotash and stew on a little hillock beside three other bowls. "Let's get sikkisuog." Maskeegsy has a flat piece of driftwood that has been slightly dug out like a large platter that could hold a lot of food. Together they go over to the large fire pits.

This is the heart of the apponaug, and it is the part that the men make. The women always do all the normal cooking and caring for everything within the villages and houses But long ago, before the First Light People came to these shores, it is told that some men had accidentally discovered this way of cooking apponaug, or shellfish. It is said that they had been fishing and diving for shellfish in the seaweed among the rocks of an island far away where once the people had lived. While they were fishing one of their canoes was destroyed on the rocks by great waves, and they had to leave much of what they had caught. They threw the seaweed with much apponaug still inside it on the fire to put it out and then started their journey to their village on another island. But the waves were still too great outside the cove and they were forced after some hours to return to their camp on the beach. They were surprised to see steam coming up from their fire under the seaweed, and when they pulled it back the shellfish had opened and had a delightful smell. Of course they began to eat and agreed they had never tasted anything so good. Later they also tried putting corn and squash and potatoes into the seaweed along with the clams and mussels and lobsters and crabs and found that everything tasted better cooked in this way. They showed the women their discovery, but proudly kept the tradition of cooking the apponaug in this way to the men.

The men have pulled back the moose and elk robes that covered the steaming seaweed and are pulling sikkisuog, the white soft-shelled clams to the side where people could take them, also the black mussels and red lobsters and crabs. Maskeegsy and Aquaya load two lobsters and a sizeable pile of clams and mussels onto their driftwood platter and go back to their bowls.

Now Aquaya understands why her friend brought both their bowls to this hillock, for Chogan and Maquas are also returning from the fire pits with a platter full of apponaug and sit where they had left their bowls on the same hillock.

Maquas looks uncertainly at the lobsters and sikkisuog. The expression on his face says, "What is this stuff?" And even, "Is it awful tasting? Is it safe?"

"It is clear you are worried about how to eat our apponaug, Maquas," Maskeegsy laughs. Sit with me, and I will show you how to handle all its mysteries, as I'm sure Chogan doesn't intend to help you at all. Chogan, why don't you share your apponaug with Aquaya, and I'll share this with Maquas."

Chogan looks at Maquas, who seems suddenly more interested in the apponaug and welcomes Maskeegsy's bold attentions. He shrugs and looks at Aquaya, and both suppress a giggle and sit together. They have been playmates since they were babies and are familiar and comfortable together, and they continue to share suppressed giggles as they eat and listen to Maskeegsy explain how to open and eat the various kinds of apponaug. She and the Mohawk seem to be in a different world, one they are drawn to explore and seems to their friends scandalous, strange, and mysterious.

For a while they eat in silence, listening only to Maskeegsy's directions, glancing at each other with laughter and wonder in their eyes. As Aquaya finishes her succotash and stew she stares into the bottom of her ceramic bowl. She had made her bowl herself, under Clan Mother's direction. She thinks of the beautiful bowls that Misesquaw molds and fires with their swirling designs made from the many-colored clays of Aquinnah. Clan Mother also made all the great vessels that they cooked the succotash and stew in for everyone. Perhaps some day, Aquaya thinks, she will be the one who teaches the molding and the firing of the clay to girls her age. Perhaps she will be the one to make the pots for nikkomo.

Aquaya studies her own bowl more closely. She was proud when she finished it and showed it to her family, but now she sees its irregularities and thinks it is only a little girl's bowl after all. Perhaps she has outgrown it.

This Sequanakeeswash is different for her than other spring moon ceremonies she remembers. It seems like more than just the end of the year. Things are changing. Autaquay has become a wife. And now Maskeegsy is acting - well, different too. Aquaya is used to talking with her friend about boys, and about other girls' reactions to boys, and now there she is with a boy - a young man, really, probably talking with him about Aquaya! Maskeegsy too seems to be moving into another world. And

Chogan, looking at her now without his usual smile - what is he thinking? They have always been friends, but she feels something different from him too now.

She has never felt uncomfortable to look at him before, but now she feels his eyes on her and she keeps her own fastened on the lobster claws she is cracking between two stones. Aren't they still children, although they take care of elders and other children now? He has not gone on his man-seeking in the forest, and she has not begun her moon-time. But the new year that begins now will bring even greater changes. She can feel it.

Autaquay and Attuck have finished eating and are slipping away to walk by themselves to the sea. It was Atookas' suggestion, as he had noticed that a numbed expression was flickering under his young bride's composure. It had been a long day for both of them, up before dawn, preparing for this, and now the ceremony, being the focus of all those people, then trying to eat and talk naturally with everyone. It was enough, if not too much. He took her hand and she followed him gratefully away from the nikkomo. Now they are disappearing over the hill towards the cliffs.

The old people watch them go with a smile, nodding knowingly to each other. Attuck's father stands and waves to the scattered people around to come closer, which they do, seeing that he has something to tell them. He lets them get seated, holding a dramatic silence.

"There is news," Espaquin begins at last, "from the Narragansett's country. On our way here we spoke with some of our people from Montaup, and the story they tell is strange." He has everyone's attention now, speaking with the rhetoric and authority of a panesis. "They speak of a floating island swimming into the Turkey Bay. On this island are small houses and three tall trees from which hang immense robes that hold the wind.

"The island bears people as well, although there was some disagreement among the Montaups as to whether they are indeed people or some strange spirits. Certainly they practice sorcery of some kind. They caused their island to stop near a Narragansett village, whereupon a small cloud of smoke came from it and in a few moments a terrible roar like nearby thunder. There were some who believed this to be a form of the Bird of Thunder, but very soon these beings on the island took out canoes and came in to shore to meet the Narragansett.

"Now it could be seen that their skin was white, sometimes pink, much as perhaps ghosts or demons might be, and they had hair of various shades that covered the lower part of their faces. On their heads and covering their breasts they wore garments made of some kind of shiny stone. They carried wondrously long knives and strange sticks with a wide opening at one end from which came fire and thunder at their bidding."

An irrepressible murmur stirs from the listeners at this. In it are tones of shock, of awe, of unease, and perhaps of disbelief as well. Espaquin gives them all time to digest his words.

"These beings had large covered baskets of strong wood, and inside were many wonders which they gave as gifts and in trade. They had knives and pots of copper, many strings of brightly colored beads that sparkled in the sun, and other things made of substances never seen which I cannot describe. From the Narragansett they took fresh water, fur pelts and hides, and some other small gifts."

"No people were injured during this encounter?" asked the Nauset sachem.

"No one was harmed in any way. I was told they came some ways into the interior, but only to observe how the people lived there. They seemed very interested in the village cornfields. Later they returned to their island, hung out the robes on the trees to fill with wind, and moved away No one knows where they came from, these strange beings, and no one knows what to make of the event. They have moved their island along the coast, perhaps seeking other villages. They are now no more to be seen, but no one knows if they will return. The village powwauh is making cleansing ceremonies of the area now."

The Assonet panesis sits down. The listeners sense he has spoken all he knows and ask no questions. A weighty silence descends. People look at the earth at their feet and shake their heads. They have no experience or knowledge to which they could relate this peculiar story. Then they look at each other for some guidance and, finding none, do what they always do when confronted by the bizarre and inexplicable, they make jokes about it and laugh, though it is an uneasy laughter.

* * * *

Some hours have passed. The sun is long past the zenith, and with its descent the wavelets of the western bay dance and sparkle ever brighter in its golden light. A ball game is in progress on the beach. Most of the one hundred or so men attending the ceremonies, excepting only the truly elderly, have joined one of the teams that are racing up and down the sand. The ball, made of tied together strips of deer hide, is darting this way and that, now in the air, now unseen below legs on the sand, as it is leaped upon, tossed or thrown or kicked amid a great din of shouting.

Maskeegsy sits with other young women watching the game. They are from many different villages, but she knows most of them, as those of her age always gather and gossip at every feast and ceremony. She knows just which of the young men running on the beach each young woman is watching, but now for the first time Maskeegsy is watching one young man herself. She tries to disguise the fact that one has caught her particular interest, because she knows the teasing she will get from the others. But it is impossible for her to look away or to seem disinterested, because the Maquas is the wildest man on the field, whooping and leaping and plunging into the fray like a very demon. He has only just learned this game, and he has taken to it as though it were the great passion of his life. At first he had seemed to scorn it, telling about the game he plays with his people at home, in which sticks are bent into a crook at one end with thongs of hide in which a small ball is caught and thrown. But look at him now!

Despite the wild cries and thrashing and speeding about on the sand there are few scores in this game because the goals are hundreds of paces apart and the ball keeps reversing direction. A few of the young women are beginning to notice that Maskeegsy is not joining the usual gossip and have begun to watch her with curiosity. They are all sitting in a circle which contains inside it a number of infants and toddlers who are their younger siblings. Their mothers are all in the cooking area on the hill, organizing the feast for tomorrow.

"Where is your brother?" calls one of the young women, "Is he not playing? Is he not well?"

Maskeegsy shrugged. She had noticed that Chogan was not on the beach when the game began, and was sure that had to do with the fact that Aquaya was also nowhere to be seen. Most curious.

* * * *

The couple in question are indeed together at this moment, far from the game, away to the east, standing on the peak of a great dune where it curls up from the probing ocean. They in turn are watching another couple, small figures strolling the beach together far below. It is the wedding couple, Autaquay and Attuck, having enough of prying and joking relatives, getting used to each other's company quietly by the rhythmic stroking of the ocean.

"I wonder what they are talking about," Aquaya says, and abruptly sits with her legs dangling over the edge of the sandy cliff.

"I don't know, but I bet I know what they're thinking about," Chogan responds with a chuckle, sitting beside her. Aquaya gives him a look, then hugs her knees and watches the other couple again.

"I guess they haven't done it," she says. Now it is Chogan staring at her. She shrugs. "Couldn't have had time. They only saw each other that once at the nikkomo."

"They don't look too eager." Chogan is surprised to find himself a little embarrassed. He's never been shy with Aquaya, but he has only talked about sex with boys. Now he wonders if the girls her age talk about it too, and what they say.

"They've got other things to think about too. He's going to be living with strangers, far from his people. She's going to be in her own house for the first time,

74

and she has to take care of everything. She really doesn't know much, not paying attention to Aunty or Clan Mother. I'm going to have to help her."

"You're going to be a good wife, Autaquay."

"What do you mean by that?" She frowned at him.

"Just, well you know a whole lot for a girl your age. You could probably already do all the things a woman has to do. What are you mad about? That was a compliment. I didn't mean anything bad."

"I didn't either. It's just that everyone seems to assume I want to get married. Like my whole life is planned out already."

"Well, don't you? I mean, what else do you want to do? Don't you want to have a family? Children?"

"I don't know. What Autaquay is doing doesn't seem very interesting to me right now. And Maskeegsy is completely ridiculous about that Maquas. And all her friends - I can't stand to be with them any more. All they talk is about men and gossip about each other! Tell me, Chogan, do men talk about women all the time?"

"Well - not all the time. Sometimes they talk about fishing."

"Fishing?"

"Fishing. Where the best spots are, what's running, how big was the catch. And about their canoes, about spears, and nets, and bait. And the weather, the winds, the tides."

"Well, that's more interesting than who is sweet on who."

"Maybe you'd rather be a man."

"Never. I like me as I am."

"What do you want, Aquaya?"

"I want to learn medicine. I want to know all about herbs and roots and berries and healing things."

Chogan nods, then is quiet for a few moments.

"What -" he began, then stopped. She looks at him and he has to look down. "What about - " he played with the sand, making a little hole. She waits. "What about - you know - sex."

She laughs, then stops, looks at the couple now far down the beach, then out to sea ahead of them.

"Well, I'm not against it. But I'm not a woman yet, you know."

"But soon, I think. And then," he follows her gaze out to sea, "Then will you- "

"Maybe."

They sit for a while, looking silently toward the eastern horizon. They are each afraid to look at the other, each wondering if the other can hear the booming drum their hearts are beating."

"What is that?"

Chogan points to the southeast. Far at sea there has appeared something they have never seen before. It looks like two tall trees with great white robes hanging from the branches and filled taught with wind, moving steadily along the coast. They should go find the elders, but they are fixed to the spot with wonder. They have not yet heard the story about the walking island in Narragansett country, and they are not sure they can believe their own eyes.

"I am afraid, Chogan."

"It's all right. It is passing. It will not come here, whatever it is."

Just then they see that Attuck and Autaquay have seen the island that moves, and now they are running back towards the village. Chogan feels relieved. Attuck will tell the elders. They will know what to do.

"Something is not right, Chogan. I feel it. I can't explain. It's like - I feel an icy wind in my heart. I don't know what that is, but it is a sign -"

"A sign? What kind of sign?"

"I don't know. There is something out of balance. Something is wrong in the world, and I feel it is coming here." She shivers. Chogan puts his arms around her and she leans her head back upon him.

Something is changing, Aquaya thinks. She has a vision that this life, the life her people have known from time immemorial, is coming to an end. The warrior in her wants to resist, to fight, but it's only a vision, a shadow. Whatever it is, her people have no knowledge of it, no medicine for it, no way to prepare. Nothing to be done but wait

They stay there, watching from the dunes, in silence and wonder and dread, until the strange being at sea has passed up the coast and disappeared from their sight.

THE DAY THE MAGIC DISAPPEARED

I am glad you have come. For several seasons it has been too hard for me to come to council or ceremonies, so my voice has not been heard. Now that I have become the oldest of our people it is important for you to hear my story, for I am the last one alive who remembers the terrible thing that happened so long ago. Some of you older ones have heard my story, but you younger people must hear it too, and you must pass it on to your children. We must never forget.

It is good to see so many of you come to visit me. Some may say, who is this strange old woman, I don't know her? That is because I cannot move about so much any more, so to see me you must take the time to come out here to my house. But I know all your families. Ask them, they will tell you. Our people have always honored their elders and listened to them, because they have seen much and suffered much, and because they carry the stories of who we are and where we have been. And from that we may judge where we may go.

There is a reason why I have not lived in the village, but ever since that terrible day made my house apart, in a secluded place - this beautiful grove of birch trees. Have you learned that the birch is sacred, a holy tree? You will know why when you live among them, when you listen to them whisper to you in the winds of autumn, and when the moon reaches through their ghostly silence to weave shadows on the snow. Here in this sacred grove I am protected. It is more than just being out of harm's way. Here my spirit is safe.

Because the evil that came to us on that terrible day was not so much a danger of death and physical loss. It is a greater danger than that. It threatens all our power, for it steals away our spirit slowly. I can see that now. For that was the day the magic went away.

Listen. This story is for you.

It was on a beautiful morning in the summer of my fifteenth year when it all began to happen. I had brought my little brother and sister and several other children to visit Grandmother. They always loved to hear her stories, and I wanted to learn more of the healing arts, for she was a very great herbalist. After we all helped her put away some of her things, and got some baskets and cutting tools, we all went into the woods. We walked slowly, because Grandmother was herself pretty old by then, and some of the little ones could not go so quickly either. As we went she showed us many kinds of plants, and told us stories about some of them, and what they were good for. It was then that I began to understand that everything that grows has a use and a purpose. Oh, yes, everything in Creation has a purpose.

Grandmother took us to a special place where she knew the sweet-grass was growing, and we spent much of that morning on that hillside meadow cutting the fragrant herb that she would later weave into her baskets and tie in braids to burn for ceremonies and healing. Suddenly Grandmother looked up. She looked like a doe listening and smelling the wind. I heard nothing but the hum of the insects in the grass. Hill after hill beyond of grassy meadows in the sun, all serene and peaceful as it had been for all time before. Indeed, it seemed that the woods behind us were quiet, but there were crows circling and calling. The animals, I know, can understand the warning of the crows, but I did not know what it meant. I remember too seeing the sea in the distance, shining blue and proud.

Suddenly there was a sound, unlike any that I knew. It was like the crack of nearby thunder, or perhaps several cracks very close together sounding as one, but there were no clouds in the sky. It came from some distance through the forest to the southeast, and it echoed and bounced through the forest from hill to hill beyond.

Grandmother stood still a moment, looking at the forest, but there was nothing to be seen. No more sound, everything as it was a moment before. Then she gathered us together and said it was time to go, although for the first time she seemed unsure, as though uncertain which way to go looking first toward the sea, then to the hills behind us, and to the forest from where we came. We all took our baskets and followed her back through the woods towards our village.

Presently she stopped. We stood silently then, and we could hear sounds of people running. It sounded like a lot of people, but there were no voices. The sounds were coming from the woods to the west of the village and were growing fainter. In a few minutes you could not really hear anything. They must have been running very fast. Still no birds were singing, and no animals stirring. All was still. It was eerie. I felt suddenly chilled on that warm summer morning, and I shivered.

And then there were new sounds. Quite a lot of noise coming from the direction of our village. But the sounds were not the kind that our people make. Sounds of strange materials jingling and cracking against each other. Feet stomping on the ground, running, but not quietly as we do. Sounds of things being torn and smashed. And loud voices making strange sounds, laughter and shouts and something like words but not in any language I could recognize. And then those sounds too moved towards the west and began to fade away.

For a while we only looked at one another, hardly daring to breathe. We waited quite a while, but heard no more sounds, so we began to enter our village, very slowly because we all knew something was very wrong. There was no one there. Even the dogs were gone. There were baskets and blankets and many other personal belongings that people had dropped in their haste to leave, scattered on the ground through the village and into the woods to the west.

They had left so suddenly they had not even put out their cooking fires. A few of the wetus were torn apart, as though someone had been looking for something, but then had given up. From east to west through the whole village there were the tracks of many, many people running, tracks made by strange hard-edged footwear like none I had ever seen.

"What can have happened?" I asked. Grandmother looked at me. There was both confusion and fear in her eyes, but I could see she was thinking in spite of that. Making up her mind quickly what to do, she told me to gather blankets for all of us and asked the children to help her get food from their houses. Somehow we both knew it was not safe to stay here.

When we had all gotten blankets and food and gathered again in the center of the village, I could see that Grandmother was unsure again. She looked to the west where all the noise and tracks had gone, she looked to the north and the many meadows beyond where we had been.

"Too open," she said, and looked to the south, where the cedar swamp is, "Too slow, too hard." Then she looked to the east, where the strange tracks had come from and made up her mind.

"That way," she said, and we all started off on the trail to the east, toward the sea. It was easier going, because whoever had come through there had widened the trail and stamped it down good. Grandmother was moving faster than I had ever seen her, and we were both carrying a couple of the small ones, but still our progress was slow, because of all the children. Grandmother also stopped every now and then to listen and taste the wind.

Suddenly at one of those stops she held up her hand. We all stood absolutely still and listened. In the distance to the west we heard faint noises, getting louder. Whatever had passed was coming back, coming down the trail right for us!

Grandmother scooped up two little ones and leaped off the trail into the woods. I herded the rest of them in the direction where she had disappeared. Just in time. The noises were coming close behind me. Grandmother crouched down in the bushes and waved at me to do the same. Soon we were all lying on the ground, no one making a sound, not even the babies.

Soon they were there and passing beside us on the trail to the sea. The same strange noises of things clashing and squeaking, of grunts and laughter and odd harsh-sounding words. I saw movement behind the leaves, blurred bits of many colors. Then they did a terrifying thing. They stopped.

They sat down right where they were, right in front of where we were hiding. They were talking all at once, and I think from the sound they were sharing drinks of water. They were all men, it seemed - a war party I guessed. I looked at the children. They were wide-eyed but absolutely still. Little Mekwa was digging her fingers into my hand.

Then one man was talking, louder than all,, and with a rough deep voice and the rest quieted down to listen to him. Suddenly, at the quietest moment, the baby Penom shrieked and started to cry. I think an insect, and ant or a wasp, must have bitten him. Grandmother put her hand over Penom's mouth, but it was too late. In a moment a whole lot of men came crashing through the bushes and surrounded us.

I clung to the ground, and the children clung to me and to Grandmother. Beside me were two legs in some shining but dusty thick hide that covered his feet to above his knees. That was the footwear that made those strange tracks, I thought, but I didn't dare yet look at the rest of these people. Pointed at the ground he held a long thin knife made of something hard like copper but of a different color, shinier, like dark ice.

They talked with each other, and the man with the rough deep voice said something. Then two men grabbed my arms and two more grabbed Grandmother's arms, and they dragged us out onto the trail. The children followed and held on to us. Many more men were there, as many men as there are nights from one new moon to the next, and they were all laughing and pointing at us. Some reached down and touched our clothes and our beads, but no one hurt us. Still, I was terrified, as you may imagine, and had no idea what they would do next.

They all wore clothes over all their bodies, even though it was full summer in the heat of day. The clothes were of unknown material and in many colors, although much of it was in some sort of heavy hide, scraped clean and shining. They carried knives in many sizes and some other tools both long and short that were like very large reeds or hollowed sticks with handles on one end and open at the other. Their skin was the most scary, gray like corpses, some with red noses and spots of red like paint but in no design just splotched in places exposed to sun. But much of their faces were covered with hair, and I could see some that had hair on their hands and arms and bits of leg or chest that showed, so that they seemed much like bear people.

Then we were pulled to our feet and made to walk among them as they started again down the trail toward the sea, where I supposed they had their canoes pulled up. The children stayed very close to us, and Grandmother dropped back to walk beside me.

"I am wondering," she said, "what it is these bear people want."

"I am thinking they are going back to their canoes which they must have come in. I am thinking they may want to take us with them as captives for their families. If they have families."

"I suppose even such ugly animals must have families. I do not like the thought, though."

We walked in silence for a while, then Grandmother spoke again.

"I have been thinking. They probably don't want a useless old one like me. A young woman like yourself and our fine young children would be a great prize. So here is what we must do. Tell the children to be ready to run with you. In a few minutes, when I see a good spot for you to escape through the woods, I will move to the left side and fall and make a big fuss. In that instant you must take the two smallest in your arms and the others must follow you in the opposite direction through the bushes and down the ravine that is over there. It is steep, and with all they are wearing and carrying, I think you will put them quickly far behind. If anything should happen and you must move faster, then you must put the babies down and go on yourself. That sounds harsh, but better two be caught than three, and the children will need you to lead them home."

We walked on. I spoke to each child and told them exactly what to do, and they understood. I kept looking to the right to feel the land, how it lay behind the bushes and through the trees, so I would be a little prepared when the time came. Suddenly up ahead Grandmother screamed and fell, grabbing a warrior and pulling him in his surprise down with her - she was that strong! I scooped up the babies whose hands I had been holding and dove through the bushes with the other children already ahead of me - they anticipated so well. We scrambled up an embankment and tumbled down the other side, scrambling down the abrupt and dizzy slope of the ravine. The men who had been pursuing us stopped at the top of the precipice and declined to go further. I kept plunging along the bank until I could see no one above us any more, and I stopped.

We were all sweat and dirt and scrapes and scratches over all our bodies, but no broken bones, no wounds, and we were safe! Only then as we looked each other over did we all suddenly realize we were not all there. One boy, my little cousin Showan, seven years old, was missing! We listened. Only the wind in the leaves and the crows still calling in the distant sky above. I tried calling. No answer. We all called. No answer. Slowly we began to retrace our way back up the bank, stopping now and then to listen for the hairy warriors and then to call. Still no sound.

When we got back near the top and called we heard Grandmother's answering call. From the sound of it I could tell she was safe! Quickly we all scampered over the hill onto the trail and found her sitting there, looking worn, but unhurt. There were tracks of dried tears down her dusty face, but she smiled when she saw us and counted our number.

"What happened?" I asked.

"I was right, they didn't want me. They would have had to carry me anyhow. But they grabbed little Showan when he tried to follow you, and they took him with them. He wasn't quick enough, poor boy. But everything else worked as we planned, and you are all here. Let's go back and see what has happened at the village."

The way back was uphill and we were all tired from running so it took quite a while, even though we were all anxious to get back and see our families. We didn't really know what might have happened to them. What if those gray bear-warriors caught them? It wasn't something we could really think about, so we all just trudged up the trail in silence.

Back at the village the people were home again - most of them. Some were still straggling in from the trail to the west - older people who couldn't travel so fast. A few people were sitting in little groups quietly, not looking at anything, and I felt that they didn't know what to say or think about what had happened. Some of the women were checking on their houses to see if anything was broken or missing, some were checking to make sure all their elders made it back safely. The ones whose wetus were torn were beginning to try and repair them. When the mothers of the children with us saw them they ran over and hugged them and took them back for something to eat. My mother looked up from cutting squash when I came in. It seemed so strange, after all our terror, to see her calmly working there, as though I had just stepped outside and she hadn't even missed me. She gave a deep sigh and almost smiled, but she went on cutting.

I heard a cry and went outside. It was my auntie Pootash, the mother of Showan. Grandmother had just told her what had happened to my cousin. My auntie was shaking her head and crying, and now suddenly I started to cry too. Coming up the trail I had been too afraid of what we might find to think about little Showan, but now I ran to my auntie and threw my arms around her and cried and cried.

Then Pootash started to ask me questions. Where had it happened? How long ago? Had I seen them take Showan? Did they try to hurt us? What can we do? At this she began to run around the village asking men to do something. They looked down at the ground. What could be done? She stood in the center and cried for help, and some of the women in our family came to her and put their arms around her and led her into her house.

Now Grandmother came alive. She marched over to the sachem, who was her brother's son, and she demanded that he call a council. The sachem nodded to one of the panesis who called out four times and the people began to come into a circle in the center, the women on one side, the sachem, the powauh, the panesis and the other men on the other. The sachem then asked the council

86

what was to be done. The head panesis, an old warrior, but still strong and very brave, said they had been taken unprepared. The enemy had surprised them with many active young warriors, more than we had. But the most terrible thing were those hollow sticks they carried that had handles on one end and opened like a kind of bowl on the other. They had pointed those sticks and a crash of thunder and fire had come from them and whole branches of trees had fallen above them. One man said he saw a squirrel who had been cut in two on the ground, and there was an awful smell and blue smoke everywhere. That's when they started to run back through the village and everyone joined them and fled and didn't look back until they got to the far hill and saw they were not followed any longer. Everyone was nodding at his story, that it was all true, just as he said.

The sachem asked the people what they thought should be done. One by one, beginning with the elders, the people all said there was nothing more they could do. The gray bear-warriors had come and gone so quickly, and there was no catching them now, even if they had enough men and an answer for the sticks of thunder-fire. Perhaps the powwauh's magic...?

The powwauh was a very old man, even older than the head panesis, very thin but still tall and erect, though he moved very slowly. He came to the center now and called for fire. Some young men ran to one of the cooking fires and brought out some flaming sticks and laid them before him. From a beaver skin bag the old man withdrew some herbs - various ones, stems with leaves on them, but I could not make out what kinds - and laid them in the flames. Then he squatted by the little fire and fanned it with his owl-feather fan. Some people are afraid of owls and their feathers, but I knew they were our powwauh's strongest magic Now he was taking out some berries, and seeds, and other small things I could not see, and putting them in the flames, all the while fanning and singing in a low voice.

Then he rose and called aloud in the voice of an owl. He stepped over the fire, through the smoke, and back again. Then he moved about the fire in four directions and did the same thing. At last he circled the fire, raised his hands and head to the sky and made the owl call four times.

Everyone waited.

Slowly his arms came down, his head lowered and he stared at the embers that now only glowed and smoked. No one moved. The old man looked all around at the people, into every face, as though he were going on a journey. He turned to the sachem and shook his head sadly. Grandmother, who was also his sister, came out to him and took both his hands in her hands and looked into his eyes. When the old man turned to us again there were tears in his eyes.

"My power is gone," he told us in a strong but quavering voice. "It is not only my power that has left. The gray bear-warriors took more than a child from us. They took the magic too."

He looked at his nephew the sachem, at Grandmother his sister, and again at us, his people, and then at the sky. He sighed and seemed to shrivel into himself and grow smaller.

"I cannot see what is coming. Something is coming, and I do not know what it is. It is something I cannot understand. Something none of us will be able to understand. I cannot tell you. I do not know how to live in the world that will be coming."

He stood, looking down at the ground, years older than when that terrible day had begun. Then Grandmother began to speak, moving about the circle, looking into her people's faces as was her way.

"My brother is an honest man, as all of you know, and what he speaks must be the truth. They took our child, and our children are the greatest and deepest magic we possess. In them, our little ones, and the unborn that will follow them, is all our power and the mystery of the future. But we must not die. Creator brought us here, to this life and this land, for a reason. We may not see into the mystery, but the mystery does not want us to die, that I know with all my soul. It want us to live, not just to survive, but to live and to give life to the world that will follow.

"Do not despair. Bad times may come, but we must hold on. We must learn and we must thrive, and most of all we must stay together and care for our families and hold on to the ways that have made our people wise and happy before."

That all happened long ago. Nine times nine summers have passed since that day, and now I am the oldest among you, the only one left who saw just what did happen. Even the little children, the babies who were with me, have gone under the ground and their spirits are with our ancestors now.

In all those years that have passed we have seen many of those hairy gray-faces return in their great canoes that move with the wind. Whenever they come it has not been good for our people. I have heard stories that have traveled the lands north to south. Sometimes they seem to come as friends, but they are not friends. Under their smiles they are cruel and heartless, they care not for elders or young ones, even babies, nor for any people, nor for our relatives the animals, nor for the trees, nor for any living thing. They lie and they cheat and they steal from us. What do they want? Who can say? They are a discontented people, and that makes them dangerous.

It was not my brother's magic only that we lost on that day. It was the magic of all our lives which we lived in beauty, in harmony with all our relatives, the plant and animal people, living rightly and with confidence as one family within Creation's circle of families. Since that day I have seen our people begin to change. They hear stories of invaders to the north and to the south. They wait for something and know not what it is, or what they shall do. But they are not of one mind. Some prepare to leave, some to fight, some to seek and follow the new ways of the strangers, some pretend nothing will change.

Lately I have heard stories of a new horror. To the south they have brought a strange sickness among the people. People burn with an inner fire that destroys them, whole villages have been wiped out, and the sickness spreads like a forest fire through the nations along the coasts. People who have escaped say it is a terrifying thing to watch. I do not tell these stories to frighten you, but we must not be blind. We must be wary. I do not know what you should do if they come, and I feel sure they will come. Perhaps we should go away, find some other place where they may not come. Only be wary. Do not trust them, do not go to them, do not let them take our children.

I will not be with you much longer, and I do not know what you must do. But I believe our power lay in the circle, that if you bind our circle again and hold fast to it, you will be able to find the magic again.

In 1534 Giovanni da Verrazzano, sailing under a commission from France, landed at Block Island, visited a tribe on Narragansett Bay, and sailed around Cape Cod. Somewhere north of there a landing party went ashore and entered a village inland. They pursued the people of the village who fled before them. When they gave up and returned they discovered an old woman, a very young woman, and a group of children. They took one of the children with them, a seven year old boy, who was never heard of again.

81 years later when this story is being told, there had been invasions by the Spanish in Florida, by the English in Virginia, and by the French in Canada. Within the next few years 80% of the population of New England was annihilated by small pox and other diseases brought by the Europeans, setting the stage for the invasion of the Pilgrims in 1620.

THE STORY OF EPANOW

The new community building on the reservation was not yet finished, but it had four walls and a roof and a floor, so the people were eager to gather there for mid-winter ceremonies. Even though it wasn't fully insulated, and there were boards where the windows should be, it was good to be in a place that really belonged to them, that was built by their own people.

The feast was over, and everyone was full of good Wampanoag succotash and chowder made in the old way with clams and fish and eels and bits of waterfowl that hunters had brought, and whatever vegetables were handy. They had roasted apples and hot sumac cider, and people were feeling satisfied but not yet ready to dance again.

Must be time for a story, the sachem said. There was a chorus of, "yes, yes, a story," and everyone looked toward the old storyteller.

"Well, we better keep warm if you're going to sit still for a story. So come on in close, snuggle up, and some one of you young fellows throw some more sticks into that stove and perk her up a bit."

"What story are you going to tell?" a young girl asked.

"I don't know yet. Let's just talk a bit, and I'll see what suits the occasion."

"Talk about what?"

"Whatever's on people's minds. We could pass the talking stick. Sachem, why don't you start her going?"

The sachem took the stick and looked at it. He smoothed the feather and roughed the rabbit fur on it and played with the beads while the others waited expectantly.

"I want to thank the Creator for this good day. For bringing all of you here safely. For all our lives. For the good feast we have eaten, for this beautiful new house we can share on our own land, and for the donation of this nice stove that's keeping us warm.

"As for a story - well, do you have any about people coming together like this in the old days?"

The talking stick went around the circle. Some people had nothing to say except they were grateful to be there and glad that everyone had come. Others had questions and wondered if there was a story to answer them.

"The sachem said this is our land, but someone told me it belongs to the state. What's the story about that?"

"We have to go back to school tomorrow"...(a groan from the young people.)

"How was it in the old days before we had schools?"

"It seems like it was better in the old days. In some ways, anyways. I mean, there wasn't all this drugs and violence and pollution and all that. So maybe they didn't have movies and TV, but they told stories and sang and danced and ate good like this. So they had canoes instead of cars, they went slower but they got there and they didn't stink up the world."

"We never should have let those boat people land in the first place. We just didn't have any immigration laws and we just let them come ruin this land like they did Europe."

"We came from somewhere else, too."

"Yeah, but we didn't steal the land from anyone."

"It just seems we didn't have any choice. They were too powerful."

"Well," said the storyteller, "now I think I know what story I should tell. To answer some of your questions, before there were schools children learned from life, from listening to the elders and watching to see how things were done, and trying things out. A lot of their learning they got from stories. Especially on the long winter nights like this. I have heard of people who used to tell stories only in winter, but our people loved them so much they told them any time.

"Of course, that was before there were books, so the storytellers had to be a whole library. They had to have a good memory and keep all those stories for the people in their heads. Young people like you learned the stories and told them when they became elders, so the stories were passed on from generation to generation, and we still have them.

"No one knows how old the stories are. Some of the oldest tell of a time when our people lived on islands far from here. Others tell of a great migration across this land, over mountains, through floods, over ice, we came here and stopped. And you were right, we didn't take this land away from anyone. In fact, wherever we have been our people have always tried to live in harmony with everyone.

"But we did not own the land, either. We are the children of Mother Earth, and she loves us all equally. So we care for her and share equally the blessings she bestows. But no one can own the earth.

"Those boat people from Europe, they had different ideas. Because they believed people could own the earth they were always fighting over it. Then they came here. We greeted them kindly, and helped them, as we have been taught. But, as you say, there were too many of them, all wanting to own the land, and they took it.

"But it does not belong to them. No matter what their laws say, they are children of the earth too, and to the earth they will return. They took our land, but we are still here. We gather again now as we always have gathered, in a house our people have built.

"Our people are poor in material things, because everything has been taken from them, but we are rich in knowledge and wisdom and the things of the spirit, because we have kept our stories, the heart of our culture. They tell us who we are, and what it is to be human beings and to live in a good way as children of the Earth.

"So here is a story now that speaks to these things. It is not an old, old story, like others I have told you. It comes from the early contact with those Europeans, nearly four hundred years ago, but already this history has begun to take on some of the magic legend."

He paused to look around into the faces of the listeners, waiting with interested patience.

When the European ships began to prowl our coasts at first they did not land. They were only making maps for the others who would follow. Then they began to come ashore to trade with our people. They had copper kettles, steel knives and hatchets, and later glass beads, and they wanted skins of furry animals.

There was one ship captain, an Englishman, his name was Hunt, who wanted something different. He wanted human beings. It seems our people would bring a good price for him for the Europeans who were very curious to see what the people who lived here were like.

What this Captain Hunt used to do was to come ashore with his knives and beads and trade like the others but he would pick a few of the strongest and finest looking young men and whisper to them.

"We have our best things on this ship," he would tell them, "they are only for a few who can appreciate them. Come and look," And when those people went on to his ships, his crew tied them up and they were taken back to Europe and sold as exhibits. All this was a long time before those boat people began to land and build their villages here. It was also before the diseases of the Europeans began to spread and to kill off thousands, tens of thousands of our people. We had never had these diseases, and we had no medicine for them. In a few years most of our villages on the coast were wiped out.

But many years before that this Captain Hunt landed at our island of Nope, and he played a trick on the village of Aquinnah, where the sacred cliffs of four colors are. He kidnapped their sachem, a man called Epanow, who was well-beloved of his people, and several of their young men.

These men were sold more than once in Europe, and may have been exhibited in several places, but the last place they came to was a very large mansion with several smaller houses owned by a very rich English lord. This lord, whose name was Sir Fernando Gorges, wanted to learn all about the world that was unknown to him, partly out of curiosity, but mostly because, although he was rich, he was always seeking more wealth. And so he wanted to know from our people what wealth might lay in our land. He was interested in furs, and in tobacco, and other herbs and foods, but mostly he was interested in gold and silver.

Epanow and our other men were kept together in a separate house. Sir Fernando managed to find another Englishman who had learned a little of our language, so he could learn from our men about what wealth may lay here that they could steal.

One day this interpreter came to Epanow to ask about medicine. It seems there was a young child of the house, a relative of the lord, who was very sick. All the English doctors had given up and said there was nothing more to be done. They believed the child would die, probably that night, and they did not want their medicine to be blamed for the death. Now Sir Fernando was curious to know if our people had medicine that might cure the child, because if we had it could make him even richer.

Epanow asked to see the child, and after that asked to be taken to the woods and fields nearby. The English watched as he moved quickly through various areas of the countryside. Every now and then he would stop, stoop down, and he seemed to whisper something in his language. Then he might take some flowers, or leaves, or some berries, or a whole plant, roots and all, always leaving behind a small bit of tobacco, and giving thanks with a prayer.

When he returned he requested boiling water and asked to be left alone with the child. People outside the room smelled strange smells and heard the sound of a rattle and low chanting in a strange tongue. The English doctors shook their heads, but were privately glad the blame for the child's death could be assigned to this savage and his ignorant and blasphemous magic. At every sound from the room, the doctors and the chaplain would roll their eyes toward heaven and pray. It was ungodly.

But in the morning the door opened, and a lively, energetic child rushed out into the waiting arms of a grateful mother. You know how quickly little children rebound when they recover from sickness. There was no sign the child had even been ill at all. It seemed like a miracle!

Epanow was summoned to the great hall of the mansion, where, before all the assembled court, the lord thanked the sachem for his help and praised him for his skill.

"You are a great doctor, sir, better than any in England. For here I have gathered the finest physicians that we have, yet none of them could do what you have done. You must have a reward."

When that was translated to Epanow, he humbly said that he had been lucky that his poor and limited knowledge had been sufficient, and that healing was only in the power of the Kiehtan, the Creator, and that was where all thanks should be directed. For himself, Epanow said, his greatest reward was the happiness of the child's family.

The lord listened to the translation with a scowl, then answered quickly.

"Come, you are too modest, sir. I declare you to be the finest doctor known to me, and to prove my faith on that point, your reward will be to become my own personal physician and care for the health of my household."

"I am grateful for this honor you give me," Epanow responded, after some thought, "but it is truly undeserved. I am not a great healer, as you would soon learn. I am a sachem, and my responsibility is to my own people, as yours is to your people here. If you wish to reward me I would ask only that you allow me and my friends to return safely to our own village and our families, for we are very homesick."

"I do not think you fully comprehend the extent of what is offered you here," Sir Fernando replied. "Here you will live as I do. You will have your own chambers, and we can bring your family to share your fortunes. Your clothes will be made by the best tailors, your food prepared by the greatest chefs of Europe, and you will have whatever you need. Your slightest request will be granted, in short, you will live as I do. You will live as well as the richest man in England. No one in all the world could live better."

The sachem considered what he was told with a frown. This Englishman did not understand Epanow's heart. What should he do?

Now he stooped and opened an elk bundle that lay at his feet. He withdrew a great feather and held it out towards the lord. The Englishman was perplexed. He should be the one giving a gift. However he did not want to offend the sachem of Aquinnah, so he grasped the offered feather.

Now here is the wonderful part - the great magic of Epanow. To the lord's surprise, Epanow did not relinquish the feather and as they both held on to it they began to rise from the floor and float in the air above the astounded faces of the court.

A great window had been left open to the warm spring air, and the feather drew them out through the window, up over the towns and fields, out across the wrinkling sea, though clouds and rustling wind, which yet they could not feel. Below the vast expanse of a great ocean rolled and turned under them until there appeared some little islands adrift in the shining waters. As they swooped low across the second island Sir Fernando could see woodlands and meadows and many deer running free and a few little villages of small bark huts.

On the western end of the island there was a village . They could see men in dugout canoes on the bay, and women in the common garden. They came to earth and many people came running, excited to see them.

The sachem showed the lord around because, of course, this was his own village of Aquinnah. Epanow showed off the great garden where the three sisters, corn, bean, and squash, grew together under the watchful care of the women who sat together on a platform where they could keep away birds and animals. The women wove mats and baskets and rolled clay into pots and scraped animal skins and sewed clothing as they chatted and gossiped together. Epanow took Sir Fernando to see the canoes in the bay where men were fishing and dragging the bottom for scallops, the herring creek and the woods and the great cliffs of four-colored clay. They toured the village itself, with its long houses made of bent poles covered with bark on the outside and woven mats on the inside, where large extended families of several households could keep warm together in winter, and the outlying small houses, or wetus, little domes for single people or small families, covered with cattail rushes that let the cool breezes through in summer but swelled in the rain to be water tight.

Later, in the evening, the people prepared a great feast, and of course there was singing and dancing and storytelling. Another magical thing was that now it seemed the English lord could understand and speak our language.

"Well, do you see now," Epanow asked him with a contented smile, "why I have been so anxious to return to my own people?" The people were all chattering happily with each other, joking and kidding each other, with explosions of laughter breaking out in regular intervals.

"I must say I do not," the lord replied. You live in dirt in these little flimsy shelters that are smelly and smokey, dressed in filthy animals skins and shaking rattles for your music. You could be living in a great mansion, dressed in silks and soft velvet, entertained by master musicians on the viol or the lute. You could be eating from fine porcelain plates and drinking from goblets of silver or gold. You could be adorned with gold and have enough to buy whatever you might want."

"Gold? Ah, I remember. That is the soft yellow metal that is so dear to you. Well, we have that as well here, but it is too soft to be useful, so no one would take it in trade."

The lords eyes began to glitter with a new interest. He thought a moment how to phrase his next question.

"Perhaps," he tried to sound casual and uninterested, "You might show me where this gold of yours is."

Epanow noticed the Englishman's voice sounded dry and thin, and the sachem could feel the man's concealed excitement.

"Yes, I forgot how crazy all you people seem to get when that metal is mentioned. I could show you much of it - but it is not here. There are places on the mainland that are full of the yellow rocks, rivers that sparkle with your gold. It lies around in chunks all over in some places, but our people don't go there. We leave it lying on the ground because you can't use it for anything."

"I would like to see that!"

"Well, if you send all our men home, we will tell you where you can find gold."

Sir Fernando agreed eagerly, and Epanow produced his magic feather again. Taking hold of it together once more, they rose in the air and quickly made the return journey in the air through the sky, across the great ocean, to the great mansion in England, and back through the open window to the great hall. The people were all standing just as they had when the two had begun their journey, watching them curiously.

"Did you see that? Did you see what happened?" the lord asked the assembly. The people looked at each other bewildered.

"My lord," one man finally ventured, "you have been but standing there like a statue, holding that feather with the savage, for the past quarter of an hour."

Sir Fernando glared at the sachem and demanded an explanation, but found he could no longer speak or understand the Wampanoag language.

"He says," said the translator, "that he could not make you understand with words, so he used the feather to take you into his mind, where you could see and feel the life of his people."

"But the gold - is that real or some trick or dream?"

"The yellow metal is on the big land," Epanow replied, "If you keep your bargain and send us home, we will tell you where to find it."

So right away Sir Fernando began to outfit a ship and prepare to send an expedition to find the gold. When the ship was ready to sail, the lord gave the captain his instructions.

"The savages may be lying. It may be only a trick, so guard them closely, and do not let them go until they have shown you the gold. If there is no gold, bring them back. If there is, you can let them go or do whatever you will with them."

When the ship came in sight of our familiar coast-line, the captain asked Epanow where the must sail to find the gold.

"We will direct you, as I said, when you have returned us safely to our village."

"We are ordered to hold you on the ship until we have the gold," the captain said. This did not surprise Epanow, as he sensed the English were more concerned with the gold than honoring their agreement. He was sure that if they sailed with the ship to search for gold they would not be returned to their village.

"Only a few in our village know how to find what you seek. I must speak to them, and they must prepare to go, as it is still far from here. A voyage of many more days."

"We will let them come to the ships. You will do all your speaking here. Arrange what you must arrange, but you will not leave the ship."

So the captain navigated the sound and anchored off of the island of Nope. As the English were preparing to lower a boat to go ashore at Aquinnah they noticed some dugout canoes putting out from the beach, so they waited for the canoes to approach.

Closely guarded by several of the crew, Epanow and his men were waiting on deck to greet their fellows. When the canoe came within hailing distance Epanow called out to them. Speaking in a dialect that the English interpreters would not understand, he instructed them to continue toward the bow of the ship and then very suddenly and with great noise, attack.

Epanow and the Aquinnah men on the ship waved pleasantly to their fellows, who waved back and kept paddling past them. They even smiled and laughed in a friendly way towards the English, who laughed and looked down to them, and joked in a relaxed happy way among themselves. It was the end of a long voyage, and they expected soon to find great riches. These simple people had no idea of the wealth they were about to give away.

All of a sudden, with no warning, there was a piercing cry which immediately was taken up by all the warriors in the canoes, followed by a great shower of arrows and spears onto the forward part of the ship. The startled

English all looked to this unexpected explosion of hostility and immediately Epanow and his companions took advantage of the distraction to leap over the side into the water.

Before the English had sorted out what had happened one of the canoes had picked up the fugitives and all the natives paddled furiously for shore and were quickly out of range of the English fire arms. The captain did not dare go onto land on the island, for now all the natives would be prepared and waiting for them. There was nothing for them to do but sail on and perhaps find a village where the people had not yet heard of their tricks.

"This is the end of the story as my grandfather told it to me," the old storyteller told the circle. "But as I have told the story over the years, knowing what we now know about those invaders, I have come to believe there is more to the story." He paused and looked around. Curiosity fixed the eyes of the listeners as they waited.

"It seems to me that probably that night those people had a celebration, a feast and a dance to proclaim their joy in their people's return. And after much eating and singing and dancing as we have done today, I imagine someone probably asked the sachem what it was like in the far lands he had seen."

"It is very different there, very strange," Epanow told his people. The great house of the English lord is made of stone and bigger than our whole village, and the rooms inside are bigger than our wetus, even our longest houses. There are many things in these great rooms, and the fires in these rooms are hidden away behind the stone shelters that give warmth to the air.

"I saw many wonders that astonished me every day, yet for all these wonders I did not see that those people were happy. The men smiled at one another but in their eyes I saw only hatred and scorn for each other. The women did not sing and laugh at their work together as ours, but seemed to be quietly suffering some unspoken pain. And the children were not running everywhere, shouting and playing as natural children do everywhere. At first I thought the children must live elsewhere, but at the end of the afternoon they appeared, dressed in their fancy regalia, and looking sullen and angry.

"I could not understand why these people were not happy because I could not understand their talk. But then I saw more that was not good there, and I began to learn.

"They took me out to show their town off to me, and to show me off to the town. They had covered the earth with stones. Everywhere you looked was stone-stone buildings, stone paths, even flowers grew from bowls of stone. These stone paths, or 'streets' as they say, absorb nothing and collect refuse, so there is filth everywhere and the town smells bad.

"And then I saw people sitting and lying along these streets. They were also filthy, and what clothes they had were worn and torn and could not keep out the cold. They were thin and seemed to be starving, some were sick and helpless, and they begged for help from people passing, who pretended to see and hear nothing. These street people had nothing, not even a house to shelter them.

100

I was shocked, because you know our people would never let anyone be cold or hungry or without shelter, and we try to heal our sick. I began to believe that the reason the people in the great houses had so much was that they took so much. They had more than they could use, and all these others did not have enough. So the rich ones must be stealing more than their share of Mother Earth's great bounty. They must be stealing the shares of these filthy, starving, sick and homeless ones.

"Then I began to think some more. They are covering the earth with stone and making it filthy. When there is not enough grass and tress and sweet air and clear fresh water, they may wish to come here. They may wish to build such towns on our land, and cover the earth with stone. And they may say to us, as they said to me, 'Come and live with us. We will show you a better life.' And then you will have a choice.

"So you must tell my story to your children, and they must tell their children so they will know how it is in those lands. Because if our people go to their towns and try to live their ways, I do not think we will be the ones living in the great houses. Even if we did, I do not think we could be happy there, stealing the earth's bounty from others. But I think we would be the ones being stolen from, the ones lying in rags, cold, and homeless and starving on their streets of heartless stone."

The old storyteller looked about at the attentive faces watching him.

"I believe that Epanow still wants this story told," he said, "because it is a story that continues, that enters our lives today. We still have this choice before us. If we accept the way that says that the earth is not our mother, that it is property for us to own and exploit, then we enter into that struggle and forget the ways which made us happy. We will fight with each other, and seek to be rich. We will no longer care for the Earth our Mother and share her bounty gladly with each other. We will no longer honor our elders and cherish each other's children and think of the unborn generations to come.

"This has happened to some of our people here on Turtle Island. So much was taken from us that many of us began to hurt themselves and to fight with each other. But now we understand that the ways of these invaders make no one happy and cause destruction everywhere, and we begin to come back to the ways of our old ones.

"That is why we are here on this land. That is why we have built this new center, so we can come together even in cold and bad weather. This is where we can mend our broken circle, where we can care for the earth and each other.

"Look around at these faces, and greet each other once more. The circle dissolves our anger and hatred and fear. The circle is our way, our original instructions, where all are equal, all are heard, all are cherished. The way of the invaders was the way of fear and destruction. We can show something better. We can give this gift to heal the world – the way of the circle, the way of love."

And the smiles and nods that went around the circle then seemed to say that this was so.

About the Author

Manitonquat (MedicineStory), author and illustrator, a Wampanoag elder born in 1929, is the author of <u>Return to Creation</u>, <u>The Original Instructions</u>, <u>The Circle Way</u>, <u>Changing the World</u>, <u>Ending Violent Crime</u> (a description of his work with prison circles), <u>Children of the Morning Light</u> (Wampanoag creation stories), <u>Grandfather Speaks</u>, (poetry), and thirty produced plays, including <u>Sometime Jam Today</u>. Formerly poetry editor and illustrator with the acclaimed Mohawk journal <u>Akwesasne Notes</u>, he also edited the Native liberation journal <u>Heritage, No. 3</u>.

With his wife Ellika he leads international family summer camps in Europe to help people discover their own ways of cooperative living in a circle, which they lost thousands of years ago. In winter they live in a small hand-made house in the New Hampshire woods and teach about nature to children. A well-known storyteller and lecturer world-wide on indigenous issues, the environment, and peace, he was keynote speaker at the U.N. ceremonies for the 50th anniversary of Gandhi's assassination.

He also writes <u>Talking Stick</u>, which can be found on the website www.circleway.org

CPSIA information can be obtained
at www.ICGtesting.com
Printed in the USA
FSOW01n1731201216
28751FS